Executed Women of the 20th and 21st Centuries

L. Kay Gillespie

UNIVERSITY PRESS OF AMERICA,® INC.
Lanham • Boulder • New York • Toronto • Plymouth, UK

Copyright © 2009 by
University Press of America,® Inc.
4501 Forbes Boulevard
Suite 200
Lanham, Maryland 20706
UPA Acquisitions Department (301) 459-3366

Estover Road
Plymouth PL6 7PY
United Kingdom

Library of Congress Control Number: 2009924598
ISBN: 978-0-7618-4566-9 (paperback : alk. paper)
eISBN: 978-0-7618-4567-6

DEDICATED TO BARBARA

WHO INTRODUCED ME TO THESE LADIES,

AND ALSO TO THEIR FAMILIES AND SURVIVORS.

PLEASE CALL ME (801-626-6245)

SO I CAN COMPLETE THE STORY.

Contents

Foreword

Over the last 25 years, my research on executions—of both men and women—has taken me on some interesting journeys.

- I have walked the "last mile" with five condemned men as they entered the execution chamber where they met their deaths by lethal injections and firing squad.
- I have walked the route the condemned took as they made their way from Newgate Prison to the infamous "triple tree" or Tyburn Gallows in London, England.
- I have stood in St. Sepulcher next to the bell that, for centuries awoke the condemned and sent them on their way to the gallows with the bellman's admonition:

> *"All you that in the condemned hold do lie,*
> *Prepare you, for tomorrow you shall die;*
> *Watch, all, and pray, the hour is drawing near*
> *That you before the Almighty must appear;*
> *Examine well yourselves, in time repent,*
> *That you may not to t'eternal flames be sent.*
> *And when St. Sepulchre's Bell to-morrow tolls,*
> *The Lord have mercy on your souls!*
> *Past twelve o'clock!"*

- I have stood at the gallows in Auschwitz where Rudolf Höss was returned and hanged following the Nazi war crime trials for his responsibility as the commander of the death camps of Auschwitz and Birkenau.

- I have walked through the execution gate where inmates were taken from the Peter Paul Fortress in Leningrad (again renamed St. Petersburg, Russia) to their executions.
- I have sat in San Quentin's double gas chamber chairs where all five of California's executed women met their deaths.

It has been a long journey in attempting to understand the phenomenon of the penalty of death—its application and process.

The journey began with a question following one of my death penalty classes, "What about women and the death penalty?"

Since that time, while others have documented the number of women on death row and how many have been executed, I have focused on their stories—who they were, what their crimes were and the stories behind their executions.

I still write with their pictures on my wall, as I have done through all of these years. I have made sure to present their lives—and deaths—with respect and dignity. I am a sociologist/criminologist and as such believe it is my obligation to remain impartial. I have no agenda. I take no position for or against capital punishment. That is the reader's prerogative.

In writing and updating this book, I have drawn from my own research, much of which has been presented at professional meetings as the research has progressed. Some of these papers include:

Inside the Death Chamber, Allyn & Bacon, 2003

"*The Last Firing Squad*," Academy of Criminal Justice Sciences (ACJS), 2004

"*Execution: the Orchestration of Death.*" American Society of Criminology (ASC), 2000

"*Offensiveness vs. Sympatisch: Why Susan Smith was not Sentenced to Die.*" ACJS, 1996

Executed Women and the Death Row Experience." ACJS, 1995

"*Women on Death Row.*" ACJS 1988

"*Spoiled Identities: Executed Mothers and their Children.*" Western Society of Criminology, (WSC) 1987

"*What Must a Woman do to be Executed: A Comparison of Executed and Non-executed Women.*" ASC 1986

"*Deferential Death: Executed Women.*" WSC 1986

The original title of this book was "Dancehall Ladies." Many, at first glance, thought it to be a book about prostitution and thus were misled. In actuality, the Dancehall was the name given to the execution chamber where the condemned met their deaths. I hope this new title will more accurately reflect the content and the purpose of the book—which is to present the human aspect of our experience with executing women in the United States, and update the application of the death penalty for women into the 21st century.

Preface to Revised Edition

At the time I completed the first edition of Dancehall Ladies, 37 women had been executed during the twentieth century and 47 awaited executions on death rows across the United States. Since the last execution, at that time, had occurred in 1984 (Velma Barfield) and the one previous to that was in 1962 (Elizabeth Duncan), it seemed highly unlikely there would be any more women executed in this century. As it turned out, however, that was not the case.

In 1998, two more women died in "Dancehalls" in two states that had not executed a woman during the 1900s–Karla Faye Tucker died by lethal injection in Texas and Judias (Judi) Buenoano died in Florida's electric chair.

I have updated the statistics and included stories about the crimes and executions of these last two victims of the Dancehall. Since commutation and clemency were big issues for these last two executions, I have also included a section on governors who dealt with these issues as they impacted the women who have been executed.

Who knows how many more women will eventually die–but, those who paid the ultimate price for their crimes during this, the twentieth and into the twenty-first century, are all recorded here.

LKG
January 2000

Prologue

In repose? Demure? No, just waiting—always waiting and aging. Not gracefully, but with a sense of dignity—if only because she has survived so long. She stands alone, isolated, her beauty forgotten. Some say she never had any. Just plain and reliable. Both workers and patrons of the dancehall call her "Gruesome Gertie." Her legs are firm but shapeless; her features could use a little touching up. The whine in her siren voice has been the last amorous whisper her suitors hear as they surrender to her lethal charms. Some succumbed quietly, others struggled. In the end none could resist.

These must be family traits. Her Alabama cousin is younger and lighter complexioned. She has the same family build—somewhat stocky, plain and strong of character. Her charms are just as fatal. The men call her "Big Yellow Mama."

Both of these ladies work in similar surroundings. They don't advertise—that would be too obvious and tasteless. They, and others of their same profession, have been around for decades. While not on public display, they wait, knowing that visiting officials and dignitaries will seek them out. There is no silk or satin, only drab walls—gray, cream, pale blues and greens. The floors are uncarpeted and the furnishings are sparse and inexpensive. Everything is functional. There is no space for trinkets or nonsense. These are working girls and their *accoutrement* reflects their status.

Etiquette books do not prescribe appropriate behavior in their presence, but such interaction is very formal including rituals of preparation, parlor behavior, and leave taking. Dress is always a matter of strictest regulation, eating is at the discretion of the suitor, and, of course, the visit must be duly reported in the proper section of the newspaper. Leave taking is done with a final "toast" as the suitor is prepared for that last embrace.

"Dancehall Ladies dance and sing. . . ."

It is the legend of the Midnight Bride that passes among the condemned. She waits with outstretched arms for the magic midnight hour when she will embrace her betrothed. The engagement varies with each person's stay on death row. She is the lady-in-waiting in the next room. The final embrace that never loosens, the final kiss that blots out all other sensations—ultimately the midnight bride consummates her union.[1]

The execution chamber where condemned inmates are electrocuted, gassed, hanged or injected, as well as the deathwatch cell where the condemned spend their last 24 hours—pacing, sweating, ranting, praying—has been referred to at one time or another as the "dancehall."

The ladies of the dancehall are not only the female names given to the implements of execution—gas chamber, electric chair, and others—but also the women who have been executed in such chambers. The description of the electric chair applies as much to the chairs as to the women who have sat in them.

Each of these "dancehall ladies" watches me as I write. "Bloody Babs" (the "Tiger Woman"), the "Obese Ogress," "Irene the Trigger Woman," the "Sugar Lady," "Sweet Pirogueing Mama," the "Duchess," "Ma," "Little Anna," "Little Eva," even the "Dowager from Tehachapi"—all look down on me from my office wall. I put their pictures there to remind me I am writing about real women, not just statistics of age, race, offense, date of birth, date of execution. These ladies on my wall were living, working, parenting human beings. I may not agree with their lifestyles, choice of companions, values, or beliefs, but I share with them a sense of existence, a sense of empathy. Their crimes were both heinous and trivial, sensational and mundane. Their punishments were extreme.

Why did these women die? Why do we execute women? I have no answers to these questions. I do have compassion. Their pictures haunt me. On my wall Barbara Graham is holding her 2-year-old son, Tommy, for the last time before her execution in California's gas chamber, Lorraine Snyder, daughter of Ruth Snyder, kneels in prayer before the trial that ended with her mother's execution. Also on the wall, 18-year-old Bessie Mae Williams stares out at a hostile world that sentenced her to die in North Carolina's gas chamber for stealing two 50 cent pieces. There are many more of these women, 49 since 1900.

I am writing their stories only partially to clear my own conscience, mostly to make others aware of the existence of these women—these forgotten ladies of the dancehall, debutantes of the deathwatch, matrons of murder—these executed women. Perhaps those who read will also share the pathos of their lives, the tragedies of their victims, and the violence of their deaths, and yet at the same time sense the frustration of dealing with their behavior and the controversies surrounding the taking of their lives.

Mine has been a personal odyssey. I have gone to where some of them were executed; I have visited the scenes of their crimes; I have talked with friends, neighbors, and family; I have read the newspapers; and I have sat quietly by their graves.

I am not a bleeding heart. I have worked in reform schools and prisons. I have dealt with criminals and delinquents—both male and female. I know the "con" jobs, the games, that must be played in and out of the justice system. I have sat with those about to be executed; I have walked the last mile with five of them, even been present at six of their deaths; and I have sat in judgment of those who violate society's laws. It is no easy task. There is no justice, only well-meaning people trying to do what is right for individuals (victims and offenders) and for society. This we call justice. I have no better definition. *But, to let all of this transpire and to distance ourselves from it is to perpetuate the faceless, nameless, identityless myth of justice!* We are executing people—human beings. To continue to do so we must acknowledge the humanity we share and come to know these whom we execute as our neighbors. Then we can wish their deaths, watch them die if we must, even feel that justice has been served by their executions—but never, never take pleasure again in their demise. The bell does toll for each of us when the executioner acts on our behalf.

NOTE

1. Witherspoon, Bill, 1968, *Death Row: A Condemned Man's True Account Of The Living Dead*. New York: Pyramid Books, paraphrase from pp. 63–64.

Acknowledgments

The completion of this book owes much to several people. Of course, Barbara Lopez for her constant research, vigilance and inspiration. Additionally, Patti Belcher of University Press for her support and encouragement. Without the typing, editing and formatting skills of Erin Gilbert, Faye Medd and Carol Jensen, it would never have gotten this far and also the skills of my graduate assistant, Kevin John. More than all, however, the patience of my wife, Marilynn, influences the final product.

Introduction:
Lethal Injection—The Ultimate High

NORTH CAROLINA

Velma Barfield—"When I go . . . it's my gateway to Heaven."

Warden Nathan Rice explained to me the procedure on that night, November 2, 1984, when Velma (Margie) Barfield was executed. She was 52 years of age and was convicted of killing her fiancé by putting ant and roach poison in his iced tea as they prepared to attend Rex Humbard's religious revival. Later she would also admit to killing one husband, her mother, and two people she had tended while they were ill. She claimed addiction to prescription drugs and the need for money to pay for her prescriptions as a motive for the killings. "I didn't—didn't mean to kill him—I just wanted to make him sick. . . ."[1] It was Velma who taught Sunday School, attended the sick, sang at their funerals, and visited their graves. It was "Mama Margie" who gave comfort to other inmates while awaiting her own death after being sentenced to die.

Before the trial, her attorney, Robert Jacobson, pled with her to show emotion, remorse, and femininity, and other qualities, all to no avail:

> I begged her to get up there and cry. . . . Women can turn on the tears when they want to, and she sure needed them then. Instead, she did just what he [Prosecutor Joe Freeman Britt] wanted her to do. She tried to fight back. I hate to say it but it's all a big game and she just couldn't or wouldn't play it.[2]

Velma Barfield not only refused to play the game, but gave Britt a standing ovation when he finished his concluding remarks. She was given the choice of lethal injection or the gas chamber and chose lethal injection.

Dressed in pink cotton pajamas and wearing blue slippers, she was strapped to the gurney and wheeled into the "dancehall." At 2:00 a.m. she was given thiopental solidum, a sleep inducing drug; and then three executioners simultaneously turned three valves, one of which released a lethal dose of procuronium bromide, a muscle relaxant that causes the heart to stop. Velma Barfield was pronounced dead at 2:15 a.m. She became the first woman to be executed in the United States since the death of California's Elizabeth Duncan in 1962.

Her last meal was a Coca-Cola and a KitKat candy bar.

Her last words were for forgiveness.

Her last thoughts—most likely of Heaven.

During her last visit with her family she told one of them, "When I go into that . . . chamber at 2:00 a.m., it's my gateway to heaven."[3]

Bessie Mae Williams—"God has answered my prayers, I'm ready now."

Velma Barfield was not the only woman executed in North Carolina, only the last. On December 6, 1944, Bessie Mae Williams, age 18, wrote this note by hand to North Carolina's Governor J.M. Broughton:

Dear Sir:
Just a few line I am ask you
will you will you please try
and save my life, if you all can
I promises you all and my God
that I will be a better girl and
live for the Lord. if you all will
please have mercy on poor me.
if you all would do that for me
I promises you all that I won't
has any more troubles out of me
I will get mysafe a job and
go to work. Because I don't has
a mother or Father or any
body to help me or care any
thing for me. I have to work for
mysafe and I am still ask you
all to please have mercy on me
and save my life for me.
Thank you.[4]

Bessie Mae Williams, Annie Mae Allison, Ralph Thompson, and Cleve Bryant Johnson, all black, were out for a good time but needed some money. They decided to rob a taxi driver in Charlotte. At the corner of 4th and Brevard they got in a Red Top Cab and drove for a while, stopping at an isolated spot in North Charlotte. As the action started, Johnson jumped out of the cab and ran off. Thompson held the driver while the two girls "cut" him and then robbed him. The driver died as a result of the knife wounds. Johnson testified for the State and was allowed to plead guilty to second degree murder; the other three were sentenced to die.

Mr. J. M. Scarborough, Bessie Mae's attorney, argued on her behalf that she had such a minor role in the crime that she should not be prosecuted.

> He states that the idea was the men's, that when the trouble began, his client was sitting on the ditch bank crying and begging Thompson not to hit the taxi driver. He admits that at Thompson's direction, she walked over to the car and picked up two 50 cent pieces that had fallen from the deceased's pocket.[5]

All I know about Bessie Mae I have obtained from newspapers and old files. She was 18 at the time of the crime, Ralph Thompson was 18, and Annie Mae was 14½. One interviewer (probably an intake worker at a detention center) described Bessie Mae's economic condition as "poor" and Bessie Mae herself as "low average mentality, grouchy nature, evasive in her conversation, Mean Sly Eye, she is the type who would allow other people's property to stick to her fingers." On a checklist of attributes, "nuisance," "illiterate," and "moronic" were checked.[6] No one seemed particularly sure of her age—least of all Bessie Mae. Annie Mae, on the other hand, used confusion about her age to argue against being executed. The records of the Mecklenburg County Juvenile Court helped with the confusion:

> These records show that on March 23, 1933, this prisoner's age was given as 3½, this would make her 15 at the present time. However, in August 1942, her age was listed as 15, which would make her 18 at the present time. However, in April 1941, her age was listed as 12, which would make her 16 at the present time. In July, 1942, in the same Court, her age was given as 14, which would make her 17 at the present time. It is noted that in the same Court, the records show her age to be three different things at the present time. Mr. Fisher [Annie Mae's attorney] explained that, in his opinion, the most reliable is the first statement, for when a child is 3½ it is hard to make much of a mistake as to its age. In his opinion any mistake of six months is most unusual. However, when a well developed negro girl gets around 12 or 13 years of age, it is hard to tell exactly what her age is. No birth certificate has been found for the prisoner. This might be due to the fact that she is an illegitimate child and that her mother was

stabbed to death when she was three years old. She was turned over to foster parents and is at the present time going under the maiden name of her foster mother. Mr. Fisher admits her actual participation in the offense but does not think that a prisoner, who is actually a child, should be executed for the offense.[7]

The execution of the "Charlotte Trio" was automatically scheduled for December 29, 1944. In North Carolina the date for execution was automatically set for the third Friday after the State Supreme Court released its opinion. Ordinarily this would not have been a problem, except there were already three executions set for December 29, and at this last hearing the court affirmed five more death sentences including that of Bessie Mae Williams. This brought the total to eight executions scheduled for the same day—4 days after Christmas.

The Winston-Salem Sentenial reported the governor's dilemma with eight executions scheduled for the same day:

> It is physically impossible to put eight persons through the lethal gas chamber in the hours between ten and four designated by the judges in pronouncing sentence. That puts a problem up to the governor for decision as to which of the eight sentences will be stayed. It requires about one hour for the State to legally kill a man or a woman in the gas chamber. Time between the dropping of the gas pellets and the doctor's pronouncement of absolute death varies from eight to 20 minutes, but it takes several minutes to prepare the victim in the chair and a good deal longer to clear the chamber of gas fumes so attendants can enter to remove the body. The entire process cannot be completed in much less than a full hour. Furthermore, it is a terrific strain on the nerves of attendants and prison officials to execute one human being. Imposition of the strain of eight in one day is almost unthinkable. The only recourse is an executive order staying some of the executions—a job that may well disturb the Governor's Christmas.[8]

On the night of Bessie Mae's execution, of the eight people to be executed, five of them received stays or reprieves, one of whom was Annie Mae, commuted to life in prison because of her young age. Bessie Mae Williams and Ralph Thompson were executed on that December 29th in 1944. She had reached her 19th birthday. Weeping and wearing striped, short-legged pajamas, she entered the gas chamber before 25 witnesses. Her final statement was given to the chaplain, "I feel I'm saved. I'm guilty of being with them, but not guilty of cutting him [the cab driver]. I did take two half-dollars off the seat. God has answered my prayers. I'm ready now."[9]

Her picture on my wall shows a rather defiant, willful black girl staring out at a hostile world. Perhaps her vision of the next world was one where she would have a place denied her in this one.

As I write, my claustrophobia kicks in—and perhaps it is only my imagination that detects the slight essence of cyanide. Those who entered the chamber are, by edict, not allowed to wear underwear or clothing with pockets because of the possibility of gas becoming trapped in the folds. It took longer to die that way. I cannot even imagine the terror that a condemned person must experience as the gas cloud slowly rises.

Rosanna Phillips—"Deliver me from this gas chamber. I don't want no part of it."

Rosanna Phillips, 2 years before Bessie Mae Williams, was the first woman executed in North Carolina's gas chamber. Her picture shows a large, scar-faced black woman about 26 years of age. She and her husband were convicted of the axe slaying of the farmer for whom they worked. The crime was particularly heinous since he was killed just a few yards from the room in which his invalid wife slept and his head was almost totally severed by the axe. After dumping his body in a well, Rosanna and Daniel, not yet married, took the victim's pocketbook and watch and headed for town. Rosanna bought a new hat and dress with the stolen money.

At their trial, each blamed the other for casting voodoo spells. She said:

That man has me crazy as a bedbug right now, and I swear I ain't had nothin' to do with no killin'. Danny stole a lock of my hair and three pictures and put a spell on me.[10]

He said:

Long time ago she went to South Carolina to a root doctor; to have him put a spell on me. Afterwards, my mother took me to a doctor near Gastonia and he gave me bag and medicine and I got over it.[11]

Each contended to the end that the other was responsible for the killing. They had a short visit together before their execution and afterward each told the chaplain they had forgiven the other.

He was executed first on the slight chance that he would take full blame for the crime and exonerate Rosanna, thus opening the door for clemency by the governor. He died quietly without mentioning anything more about Rosanna.

She entered after the chamber had been cleared of fumes. Wearing a two-piece prison "play suit" and singing a spiritual she entered nervously, accompanied by the prison matron. The cyanide dropped into the acid at 11:01 a.m. and she was pronounced dead 7 minutes and 20 seconds later. According to newspaper accounts, it was "the shortest time on record."

On January 2, 1943, Rosanna Lightner Phillips became the 256th person executed by the State of North Carolina. She was the first woman to die in the wooden chair of the gas chamber. Some described her as an "ignorant and crude black woman." She weighed 138 pounds, stood 5' 7", and wore a size 7 shoe. The mother of two children, she married Daniel 2 days after they killed 64-year-old Harry Watkins of Durham County. My picture of her is a mug shot—one forward shot and one side view. There is a long scar from below her right ear extending almost to her nose. Hung around her neck is her number—DR507. Her lips are closed but her eyes show a trusting naiveté that causes me to wonder what kind of a mother she must have been and who her two children became after her death.

The execution of Rosanna Phillips brought a denunciation from the *Greensboro News* about executing women. The newspaper, in arguing that Rosanna's death sentence should have been commuted, reminded the citizens of North Carolina that:

> Governor Locke Craig in 1916 saved Ida Ball Warren for the sole reason she was a woman. His excellency admitted the irrationality of his course, but the Edith Cavell execution was fresh in the world's mind and Miss Cavell's extermination by a German firing squad was notable only in her womanhood. Had she been a man nobody would have expected any clemency.[12]

The issue of whether a woman should be executed or should be commuted because of her gender will continue to be an issue as we examine the crimes of the rest of these ladies.

All of this is past history. On November 3, 1984, Velma Barfield died by lethal injection. There have been ten more female executions since that day, and today, there are many more women awaiting execution on death rows across the United States. The number changes almost weekly. Velma Barfield was the first woman executed following the Furman decision and the first woman to die by lethal injection. The "medicalization" of everything in our society—such as deviant behavior, criminality, homosexuality, and alcoholism—has now reached the application of the death penalty. It is not possible to know the pain involved in lethal injection executions. Early executions by this method caused the legs to shake and scissor. Subsequently, muscle relaxants were introduced to the lethal dose. Later, the condemned began to snore, thus offending the witnesses. Now, all outward signs of discomfort or pain have been masked. By taking executions out of the justice system and placing them in the medical system, a new terminology has developed. The gallows, rope, chair, chamber, noose and switch have been replaced by the IV, gurney, technician and needle. In one state, the antiseptic condition of the execution chamber was being discussed. One group wanted the chamber located in an underground tunnel, whereas another group challenged the feasibility of providing a sterile setting at that location. One sarcastic participant voiced his frustration by stating, "Heavens yes, it must be sterile, otherwise he would die of lethal infection rather than lethal injection."

It is now over two decades since the Barfield execution. Ten more women have now been executed and the increase of female executions has risen significantly when compared to other decades. Yet, the climate has changed. Some states still have never executed a woman and some states that never have in the past have executed their first woman. Some states never will. The politics of executions have changed to some extent. Some governors or other political candidates are unwilling to risk the wrath of feminist groups or other powerful interest groups to be responsible for the death of a woman.

At the time of Velma Barfield's execution, North Carolina Governor James B. Hunt, Jr., a Republican, was involved in a campaign for the U.S. Senate. A Democrat judge scheduled the Barfield execution to take place just four days before the election. The dilemma for Governor Hunt was made manifest by the *New York Times*, which reported that "political analysts say no matter how Mr. Hunt decides [on commutation], there is bound to be some negative political fallout. . . . Polls show most voters favor capital punishment, but an execution close to election day may have a depressing effect on the campaign."[13] An additional factor was the national attention focused on North Carolina, as this was to be the first execution of a woman since the lifting of the moratorium. The governor refused clemency, stating, "After carefully studying all the issues, I do not believe that the ends of justice or deterrence would be served by my intervention in this case." [For more information and a discussion of Clemency, see Chapter Seven.] Velma Barfield was executed. Governor Hunt did not win his Senate seat. The extent to which the two events are related has not been answered. Also, it is impossible to determine all the factors that influence the granting or refusing of clemency. Such decisions, obviously, are not easy. Still, they constitute one more factor that needs to be considered in studying a justice system that condemns women to be executed, removes some through executive clemency, and yet allows others to pay with their lives.

NOTES

1. Barfield, Velma. 1985. *Woman on Death Row*. Nashville, TN: Oliver-Nelson Books, p.10.

2. Kuncl, Tom and Paul Einstein. 1985. *Ladies Who Kill*. New York: Pinnacle Books, p.145.

3. *New York Times*, Nov. 2, 1984. (William E. Schmidt)

4. Copy of letter in my file, dated 1-1944, and written on Central Prison paper.

5. Memo, December 19, 1944. Memorandum For The File. William Dunn, Jr., Acting Commissioner of Paroles.

6. Copy in my file dated December 21, 1942, written by the interviewer, Elizabeth Frye.

7. Memo in my possession from William Dunn, Jr. Acting Commissioner of Paroles, dated December 19, 1944, Memorandum For The File.

8. *Winston-Salem Sentinel*, 12/14/44.

9. *The News And Observer*, December 30, 1944.

10. *The Daily Statesville*, January 1, 1943, p.7.

11. Ibid.

12. *The Greensboro News*, January 3, 1943.

13. *New York Times*, September 19, 1984.

Part One

Hanging—"[D]on't Hang Me High . . . for Decency Sake."

Capital punishment for women in the United States dates back to executions of women aboard ships bound for the colonies in the 1600s. Although such executions inevitably required hanging, women, as a rule, were not hanged. Boiling, garroting, burning, and other means were believed to be far better methods of execution for women since it was believed women were less sensitive to pain and required something more drastic. In the United States, however, hanging was used with few exceptions from the 1600s to the introduction of the electric chair to execute Martha Place in 1899 in New York.

In spite of Mary Blandy's last admonition before her hanging, "Gentlemen, don't hang me high for the sake of decency," some states continued to hang women up to 1937. It was the hanging of Eva Dugan in Arizona that brought women's executions by hanging to the public conscience.

ARIZONA

Eva Dugan—"I Don't Know Where I'm Going But I'm on My Way."

For years in the Arizona death chamber, a row of pictures documented the deaths of those who paid the price for their crimes by hanging. There were 17 in all, each framed by the noose used for the hanging. The last picture was that of a woman, Eva Dugan.

Sentenced to die for the slaying of the rancher she was living with, Eva Dugan became the first and last woman executed in Arizona. A.J. Mathis, a Tucson rancher, "hired" Eva to cook and care for him. Soon after, Mathis disappeared, as did Eva Dugan, his hired man, Jack—and his car. Mathis's body was later discovered by a man while driving a peg to pitch his tent in the desert. The tent peg struck something hard and when the camper pulled it up, he saw that it had impaled a skull that later proved to be that of the rancher, who had been missing for some time. Before the discovery of Mathis's body, Eva had been arrested in White Plains, N.Y. where she was employed as a nurse in an insane asylum, and had been driving Mathis's car. Jack was never seen again.

Eva was brought back to Tucson where she was tried and found guilty of stealing Mathis's car. She sold the car and had signed the bill of sale "Eva Mathis." Sentenced to 1 to 3 years in the state prison on the larceny charge, she served 11 months before Mathis's body was found by the camper. She was retried and sentenced to death by hanging. After the sentencing a sanity hearing was held, in which she was declared sane and eligible for execution.

Eva Dugan had been married five times and had two children. One husband was still living. Her first husband had deserted her, leaving behind a son and a daughter. Four other husbands had died, one after the other, which was curious but never brought out at her trial. Neither of her two children ever visited her before the execution. Her father, William McDaniels, living in California, kept writing to her and sent her money while she was on death row. He received the following last letter from her:

Dear Papa:
Well, the parole board handed down their decision this afternoon that I must die the 21 and I am sick and don't care much. My lawyer is going to have a trial and see if I am sane this week. Don't grief, Papa, we'll meet in a better world. They'll bury me down in Florence. Not a scratch of a pen from anybody. They have locked me up and put a guard over me. Answer soon, or it will be too late. Love, Eva[1]

While awaiting execution, Eva developed a close relationship with Warden Lorenzo Wright who she called "daddy man." He was supportive and even requested that another sanity hearing be held, before her execution—testifying that she was insane and should not be executed. At one time he stated to reporters, "Hanging Mrs. Dugan will be difficult for me. She seems to me to be a person that does not realize all she does."[2] "He was convinced of her insanity," because of her "moral attitude, violent temper, and ravenous appetite . . . Her thinking is immoral . . . her thoughts were only of men, money and food."[3] Years later, in an article for the *Arizona Republican* about the Reverend Walter Hofmann and his prison ministry, she is described as a woman whose "life had been one long binge. . . . She had the manners of a goat and the morals of a cat. She could cuss down a lumberjack. And now, at [age] 52 in 1930, she [is] a chunky, bleary, cynical baggage awaiting execution. . . ."[4]

Eva's sanity hearing was not successful. Commenting on it afterward, she said:

> You know, before I left here yesterday, I rumpled up my hair and I must have looked like a wild woman—I don't know how they could find their verdict against me in the face of the testimony. And, if I had been a flapper dressed in a keen dress, with plenty of powder and rouge on, silk stockings and classy red slippers, the jury never would have found me guilty in the first place. They would have said, "We'll let her out. Maybe we'll meet her on the street some-day." But instead of that they said, "Oh she's just an old, broken down woman and we can't be bothered."[5]

While awaiting execution, Eva spent her time sewing her burial clothing. After being turned down at the sanity hearing, she returned to her cell where she "began sewing a bunch of artificial flowers on the shroud which was made of silk covered with clusters of beads."[6] Before her death she said, "There will be none of this last minute religion for me. I am going to die as I lived. I have had two years to prepare for this. I am ready."[7] She had asked her father to send her money and with the money she earned making and sell-ing trinkets in the prison, she desired to purchase a casket. Her father lived in Ceres, California, and kept every letter she wrote to him.[8] After a bottle of poison was found in her cell the morning she was to be executed, she was searched again later and three razor blades were found in a cotton cloth con-cealed beneath the collar of her dress.

She invited the press into her cell for a final interview. After the interview she shook hands with each of them and said, "Be careful, boys. This place is easy to get into but damned hard to get out of." She later said, "I am going to meet my Maker with a clear conscience, I am innocent of any murder, and God knows I am."[9] Before the reporters left, she took up a collection of $1.00 from each of them. When asked what it was for, she replied, "To finish pay-ing for my coffin."

On the day of her execution, it was reported:

> For 60 seconds early this morning she walked in the cool night air under skies overcast by heavy clouds. It was her last glimpse of the world she was to forfeit just before dawn. . . . In the first short passage through the darkness of the prison yard, Mrs. Dugan kissed two of the guards goodbye and then joked and laughed about it. . . . "Don't hang onto my arm that way," she said sharply to one of her two guards. "They'll think I can't walk." As the first gate opened, Mrs. Dugan gave a little jump through the aperture, and then through the second as it was opened. She laughed heavily and said, "I don't know where I'm going but I'm on my way." A little farther on she turned to the guard on her left and asked, "Why are you so attentive tonight?" He did not answer, but the guard on the

other side remarked, "You're a pretty good man, Eva." "You're not a better one," she flashed in reply.[10]

As she entered the death cell, she said, "We came here to this world naked and fair. Where we go from here God only knows where."[11] For her last meal, Eva made no special request, stating, "Warden Wright asked me last night what I wanted to eat today. I told him I had always had what I wanted here and this business of special food for the last meal is all phoney. Today is just the same as yesterday or any other day as far as I am concerned."[12] However, a little later, she asked for a can of oysters, a can of milk, and some crackers. "I'd love to make an oyster stew," she explained. She was allowed to cook on a little stove just inside the cell door.

Just before her execution, one female friend said she would bring by some flowers. Eva replied, "Please don't bring me any flowers, they have always been my jinx. I like to see flowers growing, but please don't bring me any cut flowers."[13] She got a telegram from her daughter, Mrs. Cecil Loveless, saying "Dear Mother: Be brave, God is with you. All my love. I will pray for you as always. Cecil."[14] While Eva was playing whist with two other women, her hand would gently caress this letter. In the whist game she was "lucky" and played as if her own life depended upon the outcome. "Lucky," she said, "when it makes no difference."[15]

The prison was deathly quiet as the time for execution approached, except in the women's cell block. The women who had known Eva as a sister prisoner were sobbing on their narrow cots. As the procession to the gallows passed through a narrow corridor in the administration building, a woman serving time for manslaughter stepped around the corner, encountering the somber death march. She immediately fainted, but the procession continued on its way. A light sprinkle of rain was pattering on the graveled roof of the prison. Since early evening the sky had been overcast. The newspaper reported she mounted the scaffold at 5:01 p.m. and the trap was sprung immediately. Seventy persons witnessed her execution. There were five women in the chamber; it was the first time in Arizona history that an execution was witnessed by women. It was estimated that 300 people had visited her in the 24 hours before her execution. As the hangman placed the noose around her neck, Eva turned to the warden. "God bless you Eva," the warden said. "Good-bye, Daddy Wright," she replied.

The *Arizona Republican* reported, ". . . when Mrs. Dugan plunged through the trap door and hit the end of the rope with a bounding jolt, her head snapped off and rolled into a corner."[16] The flabbiness of the tissues of Mrs. Dugan's neck, weakened by a wasting disease, caused her decapitation. Five of those present as witnesses fainted—two of them men.

One reporter dramatized Eva Dugan's death by writing:

A few hours before, five had played [cards] in her condemned cell. One of the players, of course, was Mrs. Dugan, the "hostess." Another was a sister-inmate. Two other women, visitors at the prison, were in the game. And there was a Fifth Player, too. Mrs. Dugan "played a great game". . . . But at the end, the Fifth Player won—and collected his winnings at dawn. She was a good loser, was this hostess of the death cell.[17]

According to reports, Eva was buried in the bare prison graveyard in a casket that she had purchased. Reports vary as to whether she was buried in the Florence City Cemetery or in the prison graveyard. She was dressed in the death shroud she had sewn for herself. In California, her father, William McDaniels, dressed in a cheap suit she had bought for him, spent most of the day keeping a lonely vigil in his cabin, a picture of "My Eva" before him. One report stated:

If the people of Arizona believe the death of Mathis has been avenged by the taking of my daughter's life, they are to be pitied. I have no bitterness or malice against them. I forgive them," he said. Six dollars was all the money McDaniels had in the world today. His "little emergency nest egg, $50, went yesterday." His daughter wired for $50 for funeral expenses, and he sent the money.[18]

Jack, the hired man, was never captured and he was only heard from twice. Once was when Warden Wright made public a letter Mrs. Dugan had received in the mail:

Mrs. Eva Dugan, Care of the Warden, State Prison:
Dear Friend:
Sorry you had such a bad break and have decided to come out and explain how I had to hit old man Mathis. He was coming at me with a knife and would have killed me if I had not struck him. You ought to have killed him because he was trying to run off without paying you for what you had done for him, just because he was stuck on that woman in Tucson and wanted to bring her out to take your place. But you had nothing to do with it—you just ran away with me. I want to get some more evidence and some more money.[19]
Yours truly,
Jack

Jack was heard from a second time just a few days before the execution. He wrote, "Well, that was some little failure, wasn't it? Lovingly, Jack."[20] Some estimates give Jack's age as young as 16.

Immediately after Eva Dugan's execution, prison chaplain, the Reverend Walter Hofmann, spoke to the witnesses in the death chamber. "Now please take a good look and see what capital punishment does," he said. "To the last moment, Mrs. Dugan, once known as Eva Davis in her dance hall days at Juneau, Alaska, was calm." After the execution, he went outside, put his hand in his pocket and felt her dentures. Before her hands had been bound, "in womanly vanity she [had given] him her false teeth for safekeeping." "In that unspeakably horrible moment, Mr. Hofmann will say today, he felt totally involved in one of humankind's darkest deeds. What gentleness and forgiveness he has brought to the Arizona penal system in 30 years was born as Eva Dugan died."[21]

Eva Dugan looks down on me from my wall just as she was described at her sentencing, "She wore a light brown organdy dress, trimmed in metallic braid. A turban style hat and gleaming amber necklace."[22] Her last will was never filed because "the document lacks material items and correct legal phraseology." In it, to her son and daughter Eva Dugan left "a kiss across a thousand miles of heartaches," and to all who had befriended her, "heartfelt thanks." To those who had not been kind—"Forgiveness, and a wisp of hemp." [23]

My visit to Florence, Arizona, in search of Eva Dugan's grave is on a clear, bright December morning. The prison still stands, although somewhat modified since Eva was there. The Pinal County courthouse where she was tried and sentenced still stands surrounded with palm trees and orange trees. This December morning there are oranges on the trees and a slight breeze ruffling the palm fronds.

Before leaving my motel, across from the prison, I speak briefly on the telephone with Della Meadows, then director of the Pinal County Historical Museum, formerly Warden's secretary at the prison. She knew Eva Dugan during Eva's incarceration and she was employed at the prison during Eva's execution. Della is at home ill on this morning but she invites me to visit the museum.

As I enter the museum I see all the artifacts verifying existence in Florence— old clocks, sewing machines, and various antiques. Along the side wall stand the remnants of executions at the old prison—leg irons, the old trap door from the gallows, the hanging board ("slack board") and the side-by-side chairs used in the original gas chamber, which replaced hanging in Arizona. Along the top of the wall, in the corner, are 12 small glass cabinets, 8 of which contain prison mugshots with hangman's nooses around them. From her noose, Eva Dugan looks out with a grand-motherly expression. She looks much older than her 58 years. Under the hanging board this caption can be read:

Used at the Arizona State Prison during legal executions by hanging. The condemned were tied to this board to prevent possible slumping. The length of the drop through the trap door was regulated by the slack in the hangman's rope. The slack in turn was calculated according to the weight of the condemned. There was a miscalculation when Eva Dugan was hanged on the morning of February 21, 1930. Her head was jerked off. Hanging then went out of fashion.

Sometimes called the slack board, it stands about 5 feet high, is painted white and has seven pairs of holes drilled on opposite sides of the board about 10 inches apart.

I leave the museum with some sadness. What must it have been like to face execution alone and away from loved ones? It is time for me to find Eva's grave—perhaps leave a flower or just pause for a moment. I search the city cemetery, check the records of the prison cemetery and even track down mortuaries—local and others in the area—whose records might have indicated where Eva was buried. No luck! I can find no trace. I walk among the grave markers hoping to get lucky. I am disappointed. Eva had put so much stock in sewing her own burial clothes and in paying for her own plot and casket in which to be buried. Now nothing remains.

I leave Florence, Arizona, and head back home. I drive through a blizzard and slick roads as I enter the mountains through Flagstaff, still thinking of Eva Dugan. The Phoenix radio station is reporting another horrendous crime. Debra Milke, after taking her five-year-old son to see Santa Claus, drove him into the desert, where she and her boyfriend killed him. Eventually both of them will be on death row awaiting execution. And still no one can find Eva's grave.

It has taken me several years to document the execution of Dora Wright. There are no pictures and very little written or recorded about her crime. The newspaper, in reporting her sentencing, stated a jury found her guilty without recommending she be spared the death penalty:

This is the second jury in the history of the district to inflict the extreme penalty and the first time given to a woman.[24]

Table 1.1.   Since 1900, Six States Have Executed Women by Hanging

Arizona	Eva Dugan	February 21, 1930
Delaware	Mae Carey	June 7, 1935
Louisiana	Ada LeBoeuf	February 1, 1929
Louisiana	Julia Moore	February 8, 1935
Mississippi	Mary Holmes	April 29, 1937
Oklahoma	Dora Wright	July 17, 1903
Vermont	Mary Rogers	December 8, 1905

She was sentenced to die for the whipping death of a seven-year old girl. Reports differ as to whether the girl was her daughter, her adopted daughter or a girl left in her "charge."

Dora Wright, a black woman, was hanged in a double hanging, along with Charles Barrett who also died protesting his innocence, on July 17, 1903. Dora Wright died insisting the whipping she gave the girl did not result in her death.

In trying to save her life, her attorney appealed to President Roosevelt. In refusing the request, President Roosevelt stated, "If that woman was mean enough to do a thing like that, she ought to have nerve enough to meet her punishment.[25]

VERMONT

Mary Rogers—"Moral Idiot"

Mary Rogers, described in one newspaper account as a "moral idiot," was hanged for killing her husband, Marcus. She administered chloroform to him while hugging him. They had recently broken up, and under the pretext of making up, she lured him to a meeting. She and an accomplice then threw his body into the river, where he drowned. The motive was his insurance policy and her love for another man. Leon Perham, her accomplice, described as a "half-witted boy," was allowed to plead guilty to second degree murder and was spared the gallows.

As Mary climbed the gallows she removed her glasses and, handing them to one of the deputies, stated, "These are for my sister. Please see that she gets them."

Before her execution, deputies had been offered a $500 bribe by an anonymous source if they would provide her with poison so she could kill herself. Public sentiment in Vermont ran so high against her hanging that the brother of one of the state's most honored heroes, and whose life-sized portrait hung in the state capitol, requested his brother's picture be turned to face the wall if the execution were carried out.

LOUISIANA

Ada LeBoeuf—"Sweet Pirogueing Mama"

It seemed everyone in Franklin Parish was singing the song—"Sweet Pirogueing Mama, don't you angle-iron me." Even young men, asking for a date, would extend their invitation with, "Let's go pirogueing."

A pirogue is a small flat-bottomed boat used for frog hunting in the Louisiana Bayou country. Actually it was two frog hunters, cousins, who discovered the body of James LeBoeuf. Their pirogue scraped against something while they were hunting by night in Lake Palourde. The body they found had been slit from "gullet to groin" and was weighted down by railroad angle iron to keep it from surfacing. It was unrecognizable because crabs had eaten most of the face. It was the two stubby thumbs that finally identified it as that of James LeBoeuf—general manager of Morgan City's Light and Power Company. He had been missing for almost a week but his wife had not reported his absence.

Ada LeBoeuf told the sheriff she was reluctant to report the absence of her husband because people "would put two and two together and blame the Doc."[26] It was her relationship with Dr. Thomas Dreher, "civic leader, prominent physician and part owner of Morgan City's major drugstore," that had, in fact, caused friction between the two families. James LeBoeuf was said to be a jealous man who carefully watched over his 38-year-old wife, mother of four children, of whom it was said had, "borne the cares of motherhood lightly."[27]

Upon being confronted by the sheriff, she confessed to having gone out into the flood waters around the edge of the lake with her husband—each in separate pirogues. According to her confession, two men in another boat approached his and called out, "Is that you, Jim?" She then heard two shots, saw her husband had been killed, and fled back home. It was actually Dreher and his handyman Jim Beadle who met the LeBoeufs on the lake and shot James.

All three were indicted, arrested, and tried. Beadle, the handyman, was sentenced to life in prison and Ada LeBoeuf and Dreher were sentenced to die by hanging. Over 800 people thronged the courthouse during the trial. The atmosphere was described as a Roman circus. Beadle had insisted on a separate trial— especially after an incident before trial when he complained of a headache and Ada LeBoeuf said, "he wouldn't have to worry about that much longer. Soon he'd have a neck ache."[28]

Back in their cells, after the trial, Dr. Dreher demanded a cell to himself, room to exercise, and food catered by a restaurant. Ada had a rocking chair brought in, unlimited visitation rights, and freshly ironed summer dresses.

The real circus began while the two of them were awaiting execution. Governor Huey P. Long set the execution date for December 21, but pushed it back to January 5, to avoid having that event during the Christmas holiday. The board of pardons met and rejected an appeal for clemency and then reversed themselves when:

• James LeBoeuf's gun was found with one empty chamber.
• A report was received stating Beadle had confessed to an Angola prison official that he fired the fatal shots.

- A delegation of prominent New Orleans women appealed for mercy on the basis that "not only is Mrs. LeBoeuf a mother, but then too, she HAS a mother."[29]

At this point the political circus began. On January 4, the day before the scheduled execution:

- Governor Long declared he would not grant clemency.
- A sanity hearing was held for Ada and the Doc. She had to be carried into the courtroom on a bed, saying her rosary. The judge refused the plea of insanity while the two condemned wept.
- That night the Louisiana Supreme Court met to hear a motion for a one week stay. Four justices voted no; the fifth, Chief Justice O'Niell, took a paper from his pocket and read from the state constitution that any judge could issue a stay, and he declared a stay of execution. The other judges ordered the sheriff to proceed.
- The sheriff heard that Beadle wanted to see him to confess. With the lieutenant governor, he hurried to Angola Prison only to find Governor Long had left orders that no one was to see Beadle.
- The lieutenant governor and the sheriff traveled the state attempting to locate the governor.
- The lieutenant governor let it be known that if someone would kidnap the governor, he, as acting governor, would pardon not only the pair awaiting execution, but the kidnappers as well.

All appeals and manipulations failed. On the morning of the execution, February 1, 1929, Ada was asked if she would like to see Dreher one last time and she replied, "He's not my family doctor anymore."[30]

She was hanged first. He followed shortly after. The news media compared their crime and situation with that of Ruth Snyder and Judd Gray—only that it was more "diabolical."

Jim Beadle obtained his release from Angola Prison in April 1939. He died a few years later.

Julia Moore

Julia Moore (alias Julia Williams, alias Julia Powers) was hanged in Louisiana February 8, 1935. Little is known about her crime or execution. According to her death warrant, she was hanged for killing Elliot E. Wilson.

DELAWARE

May Carey—"My Way Is Clear; I Have Nothing Else to Say."

For seven years May Carey's crime went unsolved. It took place in November 1927, in Omar, Delaware. The body of Robert Hitchens, an elderly bachelor, was discovered on the floor of his home. When he did not answer the bell, neighbors forced their way into the house where they found him shot in the head and his head caved in by vicious blows. His sister, May Carey, who lived across the street, insisted he had not been murdered. According to her, "It looks to me like he's had a hemorrhage and bled to death."[31] The case was considered "a perfect murder"[32] and remained open for many years until the arrest of Robert Hitchens's 21-year-old nephew, Lawrence Carey. Lawrence had been arrested for questioning in a December 6, 1934, home burglary. While being interrogated, he was also asked if he knew anything about the murder of his uncle. "Oh, I know plenty," he responded and then began to tell the police about having heard his mother and two brothers, James and Howard, planning the murder at least a month before it happened. As it turned out, Hitchens was killed for $2,000 of insurance. Mrs. Carey and her two older sons waited for him to enter his home on November 7, 1927. As he opened the door, the three of them jumped him. One hit him on the head with a club, another used a hammer and, as he fell, May Carey ordered her son Howard to shoot him. She also hit him in the head with the hammer, later stating, "Poor fellow! I didn't want him to suffer."[33] She followed this by explaining, "Then I opened his mouth and poured lots of liquor down his throat and set the empty bottle by his side. I wanted it to look like it had been a drunken brawl."[34] The participation of her two sons was the product of a little bribery—Howard was promised a new car for his assistance.

After Lawrence's confession, he was charged and tried for the burglary in which he was involved. May Carey and her two sons were tried for murder. She was found guilty of first degree murder with a recommendation for mercy. Howard received the same verdict and recommendation. There was no mercy, however, and she and Howard were sentenced to be hanged. James was found guilty of second degree murder and sentenced to life in prison.

May Carey took all the blame. "I drove my children to do it. It was all my fault. They killed him but they would not have done it, if I hadn't made them do it."[35]

A gallows was transported from the Workhouse in New Castle County. Mrs. Carey would become the first white woman executed in Delaware and also the last. A disturbing thunder and lightning storm occurred the night before the execution. Mrs. Carey and her son had a restless night. She trembled most of it. At about 2:00 a.m., both mother and son ordered ice cream and cake as their last meal. At 5:02 a.m., she was led from her cell. Standing on the gallows her last words were, "My way is clear; I have nothing else to say."[36] She wore "a black dress with a touch of white at the collar, black stockings and black shoes."[37] She did not die of a broken neck, but rather strangled to death. Her weight had diminished so much during her time in jail that the fall did not break her neck. Next, Howard climbed the 13 steps. His last words were, "What I did was against my will. I feel sure anyone in my place would have done the same. I hope to see my three little ones on the other side."[38] He was then hanged with the same rope that hanged his mother. Their bodies were buried in St. George's cemetery near Frankford. Six uniformed state policemen were the pallbearers. May and Howard were two of eight people executed across the United States on this same day.

MISSISSIPPI

Mary Holmes—"Torch Murderer"

Mary Holmes was hanged on April 19, 1937. The newspapers referred to her crime as a "torch murder." The body of Mr. E.W. Cook, a prominent planter in Sharkey County, Mississippi, was discovered in his burning home. News accounts reported his left leg and arm and the top of his head had been severed from his body.[39] Foul play was suspected and eventually suspicion rested on Mary Holmes, age 35, who was a cook in the Cook home and on Selmon (sometimes spelled Soloman or Selman) "Dad" Brooks, age 32, both black. Both later confessed after having been found guilty and sentenced to die by hanging. They had planned the robbery for several months. Mr. Cook returned in the middle of their burglary and they killed him, returning later to set the fire in order to cover up their crime—which netted them $750. The newspaper reported their execution as follows:

> Mary was first to enter the death [chamber] shaking her head, wringing her hands and mumbling words in a very low tone, hardly audible, as she was supported by two deputies. After being placed on the trap-door, Sheriff Ewing asked her if she had anything to say and she replied, no. The trap was sprung at 12:54 and 11 minutes later she was pronounced dead.[40]

So far as can be established Mary was the first woman to be hanged in Sharkey County, and one of the few in the state.

Selmon was executed shortly after Mary's hanging and died within 12 minutes.

As I have researched the lives, crimes and executions of each of these ladies. I have discovered stories of other women who committed crimes that are very similar, sometimes almost identical, to those for which women have been executed. In some instances, the crimes were more heinous, involved greater violence, and were even more deserving of the death penalty—yet, did not result in execution. I have included some of these cases for comparison at the end of each part of this book. Maybe you will wonder, as do I, *Why are some women executed and others not?*

COMPARISON CASE:
WINNIE RUTH JUDD—"TRUNK SLAYER"

On my wall, next to the pictures of these hanged women, is the picture of another woman. She is very pretty, dressed fashionably for the time, guilty of a bizarre double murder, and sentenced to die by hanging—but never executed.

Young children growing up in the developing suburbs of Phoenix, Arizona, if inclined to play late or disobey parents, were often cautioned to be home on time or Winnie would get them. These were not necessarily idle threats since Winnie Ruth Judd was a continual escape threat at the state mental hospital located nearby. She had escaped from confinement there at least seven times, while awaiting her execution. Her story still causes chills.

On October 20, 1931, Winnie Ruth Judd arrived at the Los Angeles Union Station carrying a hatbox on her lap. She looked exhausted after her long train ride from Phoenix, Arizona. She had shipped two trunks on the train with her, but when she and her brother, who met her at the station, went to pick them up, the station agent wouldn't release them unless she opened them. He had noticed a sticky red liquid seeping from one of the trunks. She told him she didn't have the key but would go get it. As she left with her brother, the agent wrote down the license number of the car they traveled in. Later, when she failed to return, the trunks were opened and inside were the dismembered bodies of two women—Hedvig Samuelson, age 27, and Agnes LeRoi, age 32—both friends and fellow employees at the same clinic where Winnie Ruth Judd worked. Both had been shot in the head and their bodies mutilated and dismembered. (According to one source, the hatbox Mrs. Judd was carrying later turned out to contain the head of one of the victims.) She turned herself in to authorities on October 23, and was extradited soon thereafter to Phoenix. She claimed the whole affair had been a product of self-defense:

> I had gone to the girls' home to remonstrate with Miss Samuelson for some
> nasty things she had said about Mrs. LeRoi. Miss Samuelson got hold of a gun

and shot me in the left hand. I struggled with her and the gun fell. Mrs. LeRoi grabbed an ironing board and started to strike me over the head with it. In the struggle, I got hold of the gun and Sammy got shot. Mrs. LeRoi was still coming at me with the ironing board, and I had to shoot her. Then I ran from the place."[41]

Her husband, Dr. William Judd, continued to be supportive as were her parents, the Reverend and Mrs. H.J. McKinnell, of Darlington, Indiana. At his arrival in Phoenix, the Reverend commented:

You can't imagine how grateful we are to find friends instead of enemies. The horror of it all has disappeared much since last night. You know, I have never been so far away from home, and today we are in a strange land. But everything appears so bright here—the sun is brighter and the people are kind.[42]

The media quickly adopted various nicknames for Mrs. Judd—"Winsome Winnie," "Velvet Tigress," "Blonde Butcher," "Trunk Slayer" and the ubiquitous "Tiger Woman."

After a highly visible and carnival-like atmosphere trial, Winnie Ruth Judd was found guilty by an all male jury. The judge set the date of Wednesday, May 11, 1932, for her execution. Arizona's traditional day of execution had always been Friday, but Judge Speakman chose to deviate in this case, stating:

The superstition surrounding Friday the 13th is a relic of barbarism. It has been my aim in this trial to guard against anything spectacular, any show of any kind. For that reason I selected a day unassociated in the public mind with superstition.[43]

She was housed on death row at the Arizona State Prison at Florence, prisoner #8811. At that time death row consisted of four cells in the same cramped building where the gallows was located.

While Winnie Ruth Judd awaited her date with death, a hangman—G. Phil Hanna, the "Human Hangman"—applied for the job as her executioner. Stating, "I never hung a woman before," his opinion on the botched hanging of Eva Dugan was that it was caused by nervousness on the part of the hangman:

[S]he would not have been decapitated had proper procedures been followed. Hanna said he believed the ugliness had been removed from hangings over which he had presided [61 in all] inasmuch as the condemned went to their deaths without physical pain. He used a rope woven by hand of soft fibers; it cost $65, and Hanna kept it in a moisture-proof box wrapped in absorbent paper to prevent decay. His executioner's gear included three stout straps, a black hood and a pair of handcuffs. The hands were fastened in front by the handcuffs, and the longest strap encircled the arms above the elbows, buckling in the center of the back, thus functioning like a straitjacket in rendering the hands and arms immovable. Another strap was wrapped around the ankles and a third placed above the knees. The black hood was placed over the head and pulled down over the shoulders. Hanna then threw the noose around the head, drew the rope tight with the slip side of the knot against the victim's left jawbone, and stepped back signaling for the gallows trap to fall.[44]

The job application turned out to be premature since Mrs. Judd was eventually declared insane and her execution was indefinitely put on hold. She was confined to the Arizona State Hospital for the Insane in Phoenix in 1933. The previously mentioned escapes took place over the next 30 years. She was returned from the seventh and last of these on June 27, 1969, almost 7 years after the escape. Using the name Marion Ruth Lane, she was arrested in Contra Costa County, California, where she had been working as a housekeeper and babysitter.[45] She retained Melvin Belli to represent her. On August 14, 1969, California Governor Ronald Reagan signed the extradition papers and Winnie Ruth Judd was returned to Phoenix. On December 22, 1971, after repeated hearings by the Arizona Pardons Board and commutation of her sentence by Governor Jack Williams, 66-year-old Winnie Ruth Judd's final parole papers were signed and she was driven away from the prison in a car with a California license plate. Was she guilty? Did she get what she deserved? In her own words:

> On October 16, 1931, I was merely an insignificant young woman. . . . I had never been in trouble of any kind. But just a few days later the whole world was talking about me. . . . The press had never seen me or met me but they called me "Tiger Woman!" "Wolf Woman!" "Velvet Tigress!" "Butcher!"
>
> I was not present when dismemberment, and the bodies placed in the trunks, took place.
>
> However, I admit this was a ghastly deed. I've asked God many times to forgive me for the part I played in transporting the trunks to Los Angeles, but I was sick, wounded and suffering from shock.
>
> If I committed a crime it was for not giving myself to the police, since I had fought for my life.
>
> I am confessing to shooting Sammy and Anne but never will I confess to murder—only self defense.[46]

Winnie Ruth Judd died on October 23, 1998, at the age of 93.

Before proceeding to relate the stories of other executed women, perhaps it is proper to again raise the question: *Why are some women executed and others not?* It is especially pertinent after reviewing the comparison case of Winnie Ruth Judd.

There are no clear-cut answers. In their study of female criminals in England, Renee Huggett and Paul Berry identified five factors common to the eight women executed there between 1923 and 1956:

1. Their poverty which "precluded the development of their minds" as reflected in the fact that none of them tried to escape after the murders.
2. "The murders were always the solution to immediate difficulties."
3. "All were emotionally immature."
4. "All were guided and governed by these emotions."
5. "Their behavior was never at any time moderated by reason."[47]

In her book about female crime and delinquency, Coramae Richey Mann suggested three common characteristics of women awaiting execution:

1. "In each murder a man is involved either as the victim or in complicity with the woman." To Mann this suggests "that women who kill may either be responding directly to male abuse or have in some way been scarred because of a man."
2. "These murders involve motive" and the motive somehow involves money.
3. "The younger the woman, the more brutal the murder committed."[48]

In his book, Wenzel Brown focuses on six women who were executed in New York's electric chair (nicknamed "Old Sparky"). He identifies 10 characteristics common to them:

• None were members of criminal gangs.
• None had long criminal records.
• In each case the crime was murder.
• Greed was invariably present but usually as a secondary motive.
• Each (with one exception) had a highly irregular sex life.
• None of these women acted alone (only one went unaccompanied to the chair).
• Each woman was a highly complex individual, capable of giving and inspiring love, devotion and friendship.
• None was guiltless.
• In every case, the folly and stupidity of the crimes is almost beyond belief.
• The newspapers gave each woman a nickname.[49]

After spending years with these women and their histories, the most enlightening explanation as to why some women are executed and others not hinges, for me, on several related concepts. William Bowers calls it "social disfavor,"[50] John Irwin calls it "offensiveness,"[51] and I prefer the German word "sympatisch" which suggests these executed women have failed to elicit a sense of connection or empathy with those doing the judging. The extent to which a woman on trial for her life can avoid the offensiveness label and foster the sympatisch bond, she will avoid the death penalty. As Bowers states:

> The gross disparity in executions between men and women simply underscores the way in which social definitions, irrelevant to the facts of the case, enter the judicial process and affect the outcomes of capital cases.[52]

On the basis of the 20th Century executed women whose stories are told in these pages, it is possible to identify the following characteristics:

Profile

Race: 68% White, 32% Black
Average Age-38.7 (although nine were over 50 years of age)
Little if any previous history of crime (only one previous homicide conviction)
Crimes motivated by profit, emotion, or both
Crimes not necessarily "domestic" (family members, lovers, or both as victims)

Patterns

Crimes not necessarily unique nor particularly heinous
Preponderance of killings for insurance monies as motives
Male accomplices involved in most instances (although 10 women had none)
Majority of victims unrelated and unacquainted
Most executions occur in the Southern region of the United States (Although New York has executed more women than any other state—six state executions plus one federal execution.)

Explanations

Failure to portray expected societal gender role behavior as women
Failure to portray expected societal gender role behavior as mothers

Social/historical/political climate of trials
Composition of juries and combination of attorneys
Process and politics of clemency, commutations, and pardons

As the stories of these women and their crimes and executions unfold on the following pages it will be helpful to keep some of the foregoing factors in mind toward understanding events and context.

NOTES

1. *Salt Lake Tribune*, February 21, 1930.
2. Ibid.
3. *Arizona Republican*, March 20, 1930.
4. From an article by Don Dedera in the *Arizona Republican*. My copy has no date.
5. *Arizona Republican*, February 21, 1930.
6. *San Francisco Chronicle*, February 20, 1930.
7. Ibid.
8. *San Francisco Chronicle*, February 21, 1930.
9. *Arizona Republican*, February 21, 1930.
10. Ibid.
11. Ibid.
12. Ibid.
13. *Tucson Daily Citizen*, February 21, 1930.
14. Ibid.
15. Ibid.
16. *Arizona Republican*, June 30, 1972.
17. *Tucson Daily Citizen*, February 21, 1930. Delbert Cosulich, staff writer.
18. *San Francisco Chronicle*, February 22, 1930.
19. Ibid.
20. Lowell Parker, *Arizona Republican*, March 23, 1976.
21. *Arizona Republican*, June 30, 1972, article about Rev. Huffman (Hofmann).
22. *Arizona Republican*, March 23, 1976.
23. *Ogden Standard Examiner*, February 22, 1930.
24. *The Newark Advocate*, May 20, 1903.
25. *The Wapanucka Press*, July 23, 1903.
26. *The States-Item*, March 9, 1979, p.1.
27. Ibid.
28. Ibid.
29. Ibid.
30. Ibid.
31. Nash, Robert. 1980. *Murder, America*. New York: Simon and Schuster, p.399.

32. *Sunday News Journal*, Wilmington, Delaware, 12/18/1977, p.23-A.

33. Ibid.

34. Ibid.

35. Ibid.

36. *San Francisco Chronicle*, June 8, 1935.

37. Ibid.

38. Ibid.

39. *Daily Democrat-Times* of Greenville, Mississippi, May 30, 1936.

40. *The Deer Creek Pilot*, Rolling Fork, Mississippi, April 30, 1937.

41. Dobkins, J. Dwight and Robert J. Hendricks. 1973. *Winnie Ruth Judd: The Trunk Murders*. New York: Grosset & Dunlap, p.27.

42. Ibid., p.46.

43. Ibid., p.104.

44. Ibid., p.108.

45. Bommersbach, Jana. 1992. *The Trunk Murderess: Winnie Ruth Judd*. New York: Simon & Schuster, p.223.

46. This quote comes from the back cover of Bommersbach's book. She references it as a personal letter from Winnie Ruth Judd, written in 1952.

47. Huggett, Renee and Paul Berry. *Daughter of Cain: The Story of Eight Women Executed Since Edith Thompson in 1923*. London, England: George Allen & Unwin Ltd.

48. Mann Coramae Richey. 1984. *Female Crime and Delinquency*. University of Alabama: The University of Alabama.

49. Brown, Wenzell. 1958. *Women Who Died In The Chair: The Dramatic True Stories of Six Women Who Committed the Deadliest Sin*. New York: Collier Books.

50. Bowers, William J. 1981. *Legal Homicide: Death as Punishment in America, 1964–1982*. Boston, MD: Northeastern University Press.

51. Irwin, John. 1985. *The Jail: Managing the Underclass in American Society*. Berkeley: University of California Press.

52. Bowers, op.cit., p.160.

Part Two

The Electric Chair—"This Is a Step Forward in the Cause of Humanity."

On my wall is the picture of Ruth Snyder, caught suspended in the throes of death. It was taken by a hidden camera strapped to the leg of a photographer present at her execution. The picture is out of focus and fuzzy but it shows Mrs. Snyder at the moment of her execution—frozen in rigid, stark terror as the switch was thrown.

Her executioner remembers that night in Sing Sing's death house. Robert Elliot, executioner of 387 people, recorded, "When her eyes fell upon the instrument of death, she almost collapsed. The matrons tenderly assisted her to the chair, and, as she was placed in it, she broke down and wept."[1]

Referring to the picture, he stated, "It was indeed, a horrible picture, but a grimly realistic and truthful record of how Ruth Snyder died."[2]

Warden Lewis Lawes, warden of Sing Sing and opponent of the death penalty, remembered a matron had been assigned that night to stand just in front of the chair, facing Ruth Snyder, to shield her from the eyes of the witnesses, who were all men. "The matron accompanied the condemned woman into the death chamber and assumed her position. A moment later, while the straps were being adjusted, she was overcome and had to be led from the chamber. Had this not occurred, the now notorious picture incident . . . would not have happened."[3]

I have not visited the site of any electric chair executions. Judging from the names given these implements by the inmates—"Gruesome Gertie," "Old Sparkie," and "Big Yellow Mama"—I can imagine what they must be like. I have seen pictures and read descriptions by witnesses, yet, I am sure, it is impossible to imagine without using other senses—hearing and smelling. I am told one can smell the burnt flesh and hear the accompanying sounds of death. In most institutions, the electric chairs have been boxed or stored away. They have mostly been replaced by lethal injection. At one time, however, the electric chair was heralded as the most modern, most humane way of dispatching those sentenced to die. It was not a choice for those women so executed. It was mandated by the state in which the crime was committed.

Ossining, New York, in its heyday was a prison town. The infamous Sing Sing Prison brought it fame and notoriety—and dollars. It was here where Pretty-Boy Floyd, Al Capone, and others—used to hold court among their less famous cellmates. And, it was here that the electric chair found its greatest use. I have to rely on an old description of how it looked. For this I have a sketch made by Francis "Two Gun" Crowley.[4] It was described by the newspaper as:

> A large bright room about 50 feet square with four doors, four short benches for witnesses, and the chair. . . . The plaster walls are a light cream and the floor is of stone. It is a room giving the impression of sadness but for the central chair with its straps and metal.[5]

At one time New York, where the electric chair originated, had three places of execution—each with its own version of the chair. At Sing Sing it was "Gruesome Gertie." Other states, like Alabama, even had portable electric chairs that could be transported on wheels from county to county.

The use of electricity as a means of execution was begun in New York, but it was not implemented without controversy. In an age of increasing technology and enlightenment, it was inevitable that progress would expand to the method used to execute. The intent was to provide a "humane" way of death. The controversy soon involved two giants of the electrical world—George Westinghouse, Jr. (alternating current) and Thomas A. Edison (direct current). Edison, seeing a chance to promote his current and disparage that of Westinghouse, urged the use of AC current for the execution. Westinghouse, himself, was not necessarily pleased with putting his current to such use. He wanted the public to see AC current as something safe and useful in the home and daily life. He was afraid that its use in killing the condemned would promote fear and give the current a negative image. Throughout the controversy, each side conducted experiments and lobbied state officials. It was the AC that was eventually used in the first electric chair execution—that of William Kemmler in Auburn Prison, on August 6, 1890. The execution itself was not a great success. The witnesses were sickened, Edison was critical and many newspaper editorials were scathing. Nonetheless, the electric chair continued to be used. Some tried to find the right name for the process:

> The new method of killing needed a new name. At first it had been called electrical execution or electrothanasia. Edison, who'd been so close to it since the

beginning, hoped he might be able to name it. How about "electromort," "dynamort," or "ampermort"? He asked. A New York attorney proposed "electricide" but then suggested Westinghouse deserved a bow for his alternating generator—why not say a person who was executed by electricity was "Westinghoused"? The word "electrocution" (in quotation marks) began to appear in the year of Kemmler's death and soon edged all rivals out.[6]

The first woman to be executed in the electric chair was Martha Place, on March 20, 1899. She entered the death room at Sing Sing on the arm of Warden Sage. She wore a handmade black gown and was pronounced dead at 11:05 a.m. by a woman physician who "was bright looking and rapid in her movements. . . . She wore a gray gown and a huge hat with pronounced crimson trimmings."[7] Martha Place (the "Stone Woman") was convicted of killing her 17-year-old stepdaughter, Ida, on February 7, 1898. In refusing to commute the sentence of Mrs. Place, Governor Theodore Roosevelt stated:

I went carefully over the evidence, which showed that the accused had first blinded her stepdaughter with acid and then strangled her, and, after waiting in the house all day, when her husband returned at dark had attacked him and endeavored to kill him with an axe.[8]

It would be another 10 years, almost to the day, before New York's next execution of a woman.

NEW YORK

Mary Farmer—"Jesus, Mary and Joseph, Have Mercy on My Soul."

Mary Farmer, referred to by the *New York Times* as a "moral imbecile,"[9] was, along with her husband, James, sentenced to die for killing a neighbor woman. The woman's body was found stuffed in a trunk at her home. She had been hacked to death with an axe. As it turned out, Mrs. Farmer, an Irish immigrant, wanted to obtain the title to her neighbor's property so that her infant son, Peter, would grow up to be a landowner with wealth and status rather than having to suffer as had his parents in the new land. Just before her execution she left a letter to be read to him, "when he shall become old enough to understand fully its meaning."[10] While she was confined awaiting execution she was allowed to keep her son, 8 months old at the time, with her in her cell.

Mary Farmer was executed at Auburn Prison on March 30, 1909. She was pronounced dead at 6:15 a.m. She was described as:

> ... dressed in a plain black waist and skirt. Her hair was brushed severely from her forehead and fell in two braids. Two or three locks were cut from the scalp, so that the head electrodes might be properly adjusted, and the women attendants slit the left side of the skirt as far as the knee and cut the stocking.[11]

Before her death she signed a statement exonerating her husband of any part in the killing. She said he knew nothing of the crime until afterward. She entered the death room with two female attendants. In attendance as witnesses were three other women—two nurses and a physician. Her last words were "Jesus, Mary, and Joseph have mercy on my soul."[12]

Her's was the last morning execution in New York. The time for execution was changed after that to 6:00 p.m. so as to allow witnesses to arrive in the morning and return to their homes in the evening after the execution, if they wished.

Ruth Snyder—"If There Is a Penitent in This World, I Am That."

Neither of New York's three electric chairs located at Sing Sing, Auburn, and Clinton saw the execution of another woman until 1928, when Ruth Snyder of the famous photograph died January 12 of that year for the murder of her husband. [See photo.] She and Henry Judd Gray, her corset salesman and lover, were both sentenced to die for the murder of Albert Snyder, art editor of *Motor Boating* magazine and husband of Mrs. Snyder. She had previously tried seven times to kill him, including twice by disconnecting the gas while he slept, once by closing the garage door with the motor running to kill him with carbon monoxide, twice by doctoring his whiskey with bichloride of mercury, and twice by trying to overdose him with narcotics in place of his medicine.[13] Somehow Albert survived all of these attempts—until the eighth.

The couple had a 9-year-old daughter named Lorraine who had accompanied them to a bridge party on the fateful night. Returning home in the evening, all three went to bed. The next morning Lorraine heard a knocking on the wall. On investigating, she found her mother tied and gagged. When the gag was removed, Ruth Snyder told her daughter to run next door and get the neighbor. When he arrived, Mrs. Snyder told a story of being robbed and tied up. In the next room, Albert Snyder was found dead in bed. The police were summoned but they had some difficulty believing the story. Mrs. Snyder claimed she had been hit by a large man with a dark moustache and that she remembered nothing more until she regained consciousness 6 hours later and was able to attract the attention of her daughter. The police could find no marks or bruises on her head and, upon further investigation, found hidden under her mattress the jewels she claimed had been stolen. Eventually the path of suspicion led to Judd Gray as well. Both were arrested, each giving conflicting stories and blaming the other for the gruesome crime. They were tried together and piece-by-piece the real story of their crime came out.

On the night of the bridge party, the Snyders returned home. Judd Gray had arrived at the Snyder home earlier in the evening and secreted himself in the closet of an upstairs spare bedroom. The signal had been a matchbox that Mrs. Snyder said she would leave on the kitchen table if the plan was still on. After Lorraine had fallen asleep, Ruth Snyder and Judd Gray entered Mr. Snyder's room where the implements of death were used—a heavy sash weight, piano wire and chloroform. He was hit with the weight several times, his mouth and nostrils were stuffed with cotton saturated with the chloroform and then strangled with the piano wire. He put up quite a struggle but eventually died at the hands of his wife and Judd Gray.

At their trial, Judd Gray ("Putty Man," "Lover Boy") claimed that Ruth Snyder's influence and his own infatuation had overcome him and he had no power to resist her orders. She ("Momsie," "Tommie," "Tiger Woman," "Granite Woman"), on the other hand, claimed it was Judd's idea and that she had nothing to do with the actual killing. Both were found guilty and sentenced to die in the electric chair at Sing Sing.

While waiting on death row, Ruth Snyder received over 164 marriage proposals from men around the country. There were also several people who wrote letters volunteering to take the place of Snyder or Gray in the electric chair.

Ruth Snyder and Judd Gray each had spent time before the execution visiting with their families. Each had a daughter of the same age, neither of whom was allowed to visit in the prison. Judd Gray left 11 letters with the warden, one to be given to his daughter Judy on each birthday (August 25) until she was 21. Ruth Snyder left a letter with her mother to be given to her daughter Lorraine, "when she is old enough to understand it."[14]

Mrs. Snyder died first. It had been Warden Lawes's policy that when there were to be multiple executions, to have the weaker of the two executed first. Ruth Snyder entered the chamber accompanied by the Catholic chaplain. She had converted from the Lutheran to Catholic religion while she was awaiting trial. Before leaving her cell she said, "If there is a penitent in this world, I am that. . . . I am very, very sorry. I have sinned and I am paying dearly for it. I only hope that my life—that I am giving up now—will serve as a lesson to the world."[15] She was quickly strapped in the chair. Her last words were "Father forgive them, for they know not what they do." Only one jolt of electricity was given at 11:01 p.m. The warden had ordered the switch thrown only once to dispel a rumor that the condemned was not killed as a result of the electricity but rather later as a result of the mandatory autopsy. In the case of Ruth Snyder, her mother, brother, and attorney had requested they be given the body immediately after the execution, and that no autopsy be held, believing they could deliver it to a physician who would inject it with adrenalin and restore it to life. This was not allowed and Mrs. Snyder was pronounced dead at 11:04 p.m.

Although this request may seem unusual, there had been other attempts at resuscitation after execution in the United States. One case was that of Salvatore Cardinella in Illinois. Cardinella was convicted of the murder of a saloonkeeper during a holdup. He was hanged on April 15, 1921. Before his hanging he made arrangements for his body to be claimed immediately afterward and to be put into a casket with a hot water mattress and lined with hot water bottles. This casket would then be taken by ambulance, equipped with resuscitation devices, and staffed by physicians and nurses who would then give hypodermic injections and oxygen to restore him to life.

> No sooner had Cardinella been pronounced dead by the jail physician, than his body—with a scarlet circle around the neck—was placed in a wicker-basket coffin and rushed to an ambulance waiting in the jail yard. Once the casket was loaded aboard, a jail guard saw a woman in nurse's garb and two men who appeared to be doctors spring into action. As the ambulance moved away, the woman began to frantically rub Cardinella's wrists, while the "doctors" began to administer hypodermic injections.
>
> The guard alerted police who overtook the ambulance and brought it back to the jail yard. In it jailers found the casket equipped with a rubber mattress full of hot water, and hot water bottles; an oxygen tank; an electrical battery; hypodermic syringes and other paraphernalia. The ambulance was delayed for an hour, while Cardinella's body grew cold and rigor mortis began to set in. Dr. Francis W. made sure Cardinella was dead beyond recall before the ambulance was finally permitted to go on its way.[16]

It may seem that this was an extreme case of paranoia on the part of the officials; however, it was the concerns of an Illinois judge that caused them to be so careful. It was the judge's opinion that:

> Once a man had been pronounced dead, he was indeed legally dead. If he was revived after being declared dead . . . he could go out and commit any crime that struck his fancy, without fear of punishment, because technically a dead man is a non-person—and thus immune from the law.[17]

Judd Gray followed Ruth Snyder to the chair and was pronounced dead 10 minutes later. His last words to the warden were, "I hope that my example will be a warning to others and that some who are going wrong will change the rudder and keep off the rocks."[18]

New York law required that the clothing worn by those executed be burned immediately after execution.

Of all the executed women, Ruth Snyder is probably the one most recognized. Her's is the only one ever captured on film. The picture, captured the moment the switch was thrown, ran on the front page of the *New York Daily News* the day after her execution. For some people this picture encapsulates the horror of the electric chair. Elaborate precautions were put in place, and still exist, to be sure such a picture is never again taken. But, this one time, coincidence and circumstance combined and were juxtaposed in such a way that Thomas Howard, on special assignment to the *Daily News*, could take the picture.

Apparently, Howard had rushed into the execution chamber to obtain a front row seat. Strapped to his left leg ankle was a small camera which was concealed by his pants leg. At the moment of execution he pressed a plunger that had been run up his leg to his pocket, thus allowing him to take the picture. It was only by the greatest coincidence that the matron, who would have been standing directly in front of him, had to leave the chamber before the execution.

There are many who believe participating in an execution would be no big deal. However, in the case of this execution particularly, there were rumors that the executioner, Robert Elliot, had a breakdown. In his book, *Agent of Death*, Elliot denied this.

> In the death chamber . . . I made the usual preparations. I had brought my own electrodes for use on Mrs. Snyder. While I awaited the arrival of the officers and the witnesses, a feeling of repulsion swept over me. I was to send a woman, a mother, into eternity. The more I permitted my mind to dwell upon it, the more it cut deep into my heart. But I also realized that this woman had murdered; that the law demanded her life for the one she had so cruelly taken.[19]
>
> Shortly after the execution was over, I left the prison for home. My wife was waiting for me, but she asked no questions. Though it was very late, I read for an hour before going to bed. I wanted to erase the thought of my night's work.[20]

Warden Lawes left the state and traveled to Florida, accompanied by his physician, to recover from his own breakdown. In his memoirs he wrote of one particular letter of comfort he received:

> I was grateful to Ruth Hale, one of America's foremost women of letters, for her telegram: "Have tried all day to phone you but you very sensibly do not answer. I have wanted to say that my heart is heavy with yours and that since you do this hideous job for all of us, I would take my part if I could."[21]

Anna Antonio—"I Am Not Afraid to Die.
I Have Nothing on My Conscience."

"Little Anna" died in the same electric chair on August 9, 1934. She was age 29 and the mother of three children. Actually there had been a fourth child who died because of the brutality of her husband, Salvatore Antonio. Their marriage had been a stormy one and Anna claimed he was cruel and abusive and that the house "was always full of dope and guns." Salvatore's body was found dumped alongside a country road. He had been shot five times and stabbed 15 times. Vincent Saetta and Sam Faracci, two of his associates, were arrested for the murder. When they finally confessed, both implicated Anna Antonio. They claimed she had hired them to kill her husband and promised to pay them from the $5,000 insurance policy that he carried. Anna, proclaiming her innocence, said, "I did not tell those men to kill my husband for his insurance money. . . . I could have killed him a dozen times. . . . One of these men came to me and said they were going to kill my husband, and I said: 'I do not care what happens to my husband, I care only for my three children.'"[22] The three children were Frank, age 3; Phyllis, age 9; and Marie, age 6, who turned 7 on the day of her mother's execution.

All three conspirators were sentenced to die. During the last 6 weeks before the actual execution, three different reprieves were granted. The reason for one was a statement by a prison clerk that he heard Saetta state he was using Anna in an attempt to escape the chair. According to this clerk, Saetta had bragged, "They'll never send me to the hot seat. Not while there's a dame in the case. In New York they don't like to send a woman to the chair and they can't send me and not her."[23] Later, in an attempt to spare Anna, Saetta signed a statement:

> I make this affidavit of my own free will without promise or hope of reward. I make it in the interest of justice for use upon application for a new trial for Mrs. Anna Antonio, whom I know to be innocent of the crime of which she is convicted. I know the facts to be that Mrs. Antonio in no way asked me to kill her husband, in no way encouraged me to kill her husband and never at any time promised me any money to kill her husband.[24]

Neither this belated admission nor any of the reprieves resulted in a new trial and the date for execution was set for August 9, 1934. Anna spent the day with her children. She made a dress for her daughter's birthday and played ball with all three children in the women's courtyard at Sing Sing. Expecting to be reprieved again, she refused to tell the children a final farewell and even refused a last meal. When the warden came to get her, she was totally surprised. Wearing a dress she had made herself, it was described by Robert Elliot, her executioner, as "blue with bits of white trimming on the sleeves and across the front."[25] There was a 10-minute wait, as someone had started her too early. During this wait she stood trembling in the outer corridor. Finally, after being allowed to proceed, she was strapped in the chair at 10:12 p.m. and pronounced dead at 10:16 p.m. She was followed by a "surly" Sam Faracci, father of 10 children, and then by Vincent Saetta, who was described in newspaper accounts variously as "death house gallant," "speaker of the beautiful lie," and "gay knight of the death house."

Anna Antonio's son, Frankie, was taken and cared for by her brother. The two daughters went to the "orphan's home" and her pet canary, which the warden had allowed her to keep in her cell, was apparently given to another inmate. In a statement after the executions, Governor Herbert H. Lehman said:

> Appeals have been made to me to grant executive clemency to Anna Antonio on account of her sex, but the law makes no distinction of sex in the punishment of crime; nor would my own conscience or the duty imposed upon me by my oath of office permit me to do so.[26]

Little Anna became the fourth woman executed by electric chair in New York.

Eva Coo—"I Wish to God the Men I Know Would Help Me Now."

The plain chair in the yellow-walled execution chamber took its next victim less than a year later. This time, "Little Eva" died wearing a blue print dress and proclaiming her innocence to the end. "I wish to God the men I know would help me now," was her complaint to reporter Dorothy Kilgallen, who covered her trial.[27]

The press dubbed her Little Eva after the heroine in *Uncle Tom's Cabin*. The nickname stuck. Eva Coo, the oldest of six daughters, born in Haliburton, Ontario, Canada, was the owner and operator of Woodbine Inn just outside Cooperstown, New York. The inn was known for its rowdiness and for its powerful visitors. Of Eva, a deputy sheriff said, "She was a big hearted woman. Everybody visited her place, even a minister. She took their money and let them have their fun—politicians, doctors and lawyers."[28] Eva was tried and found guilty of the murder of "Gimpy" (Harry Wright), her crippled handyman, whom she had promised to take care of after his mother's death. Gimpy was 53 years old but his insurance policy promised double benefits if he died before the age of 50. Eva Coo was charged with altering his birth date and then, in the company of Martha Clift, one of her "hostesses" at the inn, hitting him with a mallet and running over him with an automobile on Crumhorn Mountain. To coerce a confession from her, the police dug up Gimpy's body and had Eva reenact the crime with his dead corpse. According to her attorney:

> In that re-enactment . . . Wright's body, removed from the grave "without a court order" six days after his death, was taken from its coffin and suddenly thrust before the road-house keeper [Eva Coo]. "She was forced to take hold of that body and lift it up."[29]

Martha Clift, who actually drove the car over Gimpy, testified against Eva in return for immunity on the condition she would tell the truth. (Martha actually lied at one time, lost her immunity, and was found guilty of second degree murder.)

The trial was well publicized and well attended. One enterprising man sold souvenirs outside the courthouse with the pitch, "Only a quarter, folks. . . . Made out of wood from the haunted house on Crumhorn Mountain. . . . Buy a mallet like the one Eva Coo used in the murder of Gimpy Wright."[30]

Eva maintained her innocence:

> I know secrets about a lot of well-known men around here. I know about things they did when their wives weren't around, and I might have to tell a few of them, now that I am down and they are stepping on me. Some of the biggest shots in the county came down to my place on Saturday nights.
>
> They say my place was pretty wild. I didn't do anything to make it that way. It was the men of the county who did it. I took care of Harry Wright for four years after his mother died. They say I killed him. It's a damn vicious lie.[31]

The trial, although starting slowly, soon resembled a circus:

> Each day the crowd grew larger and more unruly. They trampled down the lawn between the courthouse and the jail, brought picnic lunches to eat on the shores of Lake Otsego, and vied with one another to secure tickets of admission to the courtroom. A brisk market in tickets sprang up in spite of Judge Heath's warning that the sale was illegal, and that any person apprehended in the making of such a sale would be prosecuted.[32]

In spite of her insistence of her innocence, Eva Coo was found guilty and sentenced to die, and Martha Clift was sentenced to 20 years to life.

At Sing Sing, Little Eva lost weight and interest. She described herself for the press as:

> Short and stocky and I've gotten kind of flabby . . . my ankles always were thick and my hands are rough and knotted from working on the farm . . . my neck is

thick and my skin rough with big pores. Jess used to say the nicest thing about me were my eyes.[33]

On the day of her execution she refused a final meal, anticipating there would be a last minute reprieve. Because of this belief, she also refused to see her family. For all intents, she had been dead to them for 17 years, but having read of her situation in the papers, they tried to make contact again. She refused to see them, waiting to meet them again in better circumstances outside of the prison. The newspaper explained:

> She did not want them to see her with her blonde hair graying and her face drawn and lined. Her refusal to see them "in this condition" she told them was "for your sake."[34]

Eva Coo died in the electric chair at Sing Sing on the evening of June 27, 1935. She was wearing a blue dress with a red and white flowered pattern. She was pronounced dead at 11:07 p.m. Warden Lawes summed up his feelings in a statement after her execution:

> I don't know if she was innocent or guilty. But I do know that she got a rotten deal all around. Rotten. She told me that after her arrest she signed a power of attorney for a lawyer so that he could collect three thousand dollars a man owed her. She gave them everything to defend her. I suppose I ought not to say anything. My job was to kill that woman, not defend her. And I'm not defending her—she may be guilty as well, but she got a raw deal. Her trial attorneys—do you know what they did to help her lately? Know what? One of them wrote to me, saying he'd like four invitations to her execution. That's the kind of defense she had.[35]

What became of Martha Clift, mother of two children ages 5 and 6 and hostess at the Woodbine Inn, to whom Eva pled, "If only Mrs. Clift would tell the truth I would be saved."[36] What became of her? Eva stated before her execution, "She more than anyone else is sending me to the chair. She'll get her punishment from God, but I can't hate her. . . ."[37] Martha Clift was paroled from the Bedford Hills prison 13 years after Eva was executed. The man who prosecuted her had since been appointed to the parole board and cast his vote in favor of her parole. Perhaps it was as Eva said, "I guess Little Eva was never in line for a break."[38]

Mary Francis Creighton—"I'm Tired, Maybe I Can Rest Now."

Her husband called her "Fanny." The press called her a "modern Lucretia Borgia." Mary Francis Creighton never saw the execution chamber (now repainted and referred to as the "green room"), nor did she see the chair. Ten men had gone to their deaths since her arrival and she watched each of them as they passed her cell. But now that it was her turn, she was totally unconscious. She was wheeled into the room in a wheelchair by two matrons and three guards. They formed a protective screen around her as she was strapped into the chair. This was done to prevent pictures and to shield her from the male witnesses. She wore a pink crepe nightgown and a black satin kimono. One news report described her as showing "no life whatever . . . Twenty-four official witnesses agreed she was unconscious. Her head lolled limply over her right shoulder. Her eyes were closed. Her fat cheeks, once notable for their rosy color but now chalk white, sagged heavily into the creases of her neck."[39]

Mrs. Creighton and her lover Edward Applegate were found guilty and sentenced to die for poisoning Applegate's 300 pound wife. The Creightons and Applegates had lived together to save money. As it turned out Applegate had been carrying on an affair with both Mrs. Creighton and her 15-year-old daughter Ruth. Mrs. Applegate had to be eliminated to pave the way for Edward ("Uncle Ev") to marry Ruth. Her death was accomplished with Rough on Rats brand rat poison in a glass of eggnog. Each blamed the other for actually administering the dose. Both were sentenced to die.

Mrs. Creighton was no stranger to murder charges. She and her husband had been tried 10 years earlier for the poison death of her 18-year-old crippled brother. They were acquitted and Mary Francis was tried alone for the poison deaths of her husband's parents. She was also acquitted of these deaths. Some court watchers believed the acquittals were probably the result of sympathy for Mrs. Creighton, who gave birth to her second child, a son, in jail while awaiting trial.

It was these earlier trials that caused suspicion to fall on Mrs. Creighton after the death of Mrs. Applegate. An anonymous letter signed "A Friend of Justice" was sent to the police. It informed the police of the earlier trials and suggested they look into the death of Ada Applegate. It closed, "Will you please go quietly and catch this friend at work?" The subsequent autopsy revealed arsenic poison and resulted in the charges of murder. There were some who believed Mrs. Creighton dragged Applegate into his involvement and that he was not guilty of the murder itself. Mrs. Creighton was scheduled to be executed first in the hopes that she might exonerate Edward at the last minute.

On the day of her execution, Mary Francis Creighton refused to see her two children (Ruth, age 16 and John Jr. "Jackie," age 10). She did say goodbye to her husband who continued to believe in her innocence. Her last meal was a dish of ice cream. She was accompanied by a Catholic priest to her execution.

Just that afternoon she had been baptized a Catholic. Thirty minutes before her execution she passed out, never to regain consciousness. She was the first person ever to have been totally unconcious when executed in New York's electric chair.

Helen Fowler—"Black Helen," "Sugar Woman"

Helen Fowler was executed at Sing Sing on November 16, 1944. It was an unusually uneventful execution. The warden even had to solicit volunteers to round up enough witnesses for the execution. Even the newspapers were quiet. One editor commented:

> Why should we have run the story? Why waste space on the last words of a woman like her or bother to tell what she ate for her final meal? It wouldn't have been worthwhile. There just aren't enough people who care what happens to a woman like Helen Fowler.[40]

She ate the regular prison meal before her death and left no recorded last words. She died with her accomplice and common-law husband George Knight, 10 years her junior. Three of her children testified against her at her trial and she became the only black woman executed for felony murder in the state of New York.

Helen Fowler—"Black Helen," "The Sugar Woman"—lived in the red light district of Niagara Falls. She had at least four children (possibly more) from as many fathers. She was found guilty of killing George Fowler, a 63-year-old white man. He had taken a wad of money into the "colored district" where he bought drinks and bragged of his money. Fowler and Knight were accused of beating him with a hammer and kicking him to death. They were tried together in an atmosphere of racial prejudice and a war-related industrial boom that brought an increased black population into the Niagara Falls community.

The seven-man, five-woman jury found both black defendants guilty of killing and robbing their white victim. It was not a surprise. Even Helen's attorney found it difficult to mount much of a defense. In his summation he stated:

> It is hard to make an argument for Helen Fowler. She is guilty of so many things on this record. She is guilty of any number of crimes and yet she is not being tried for them, but for murder in the first degree. She has been handed from man to man, has had children by them all. She has lied; she has cheated; she has sold herself. Perhaps it would be better for her children if she were put out of the way, but I would rather leave the issue to the Good Lord.[41]

Martha Jule Beck—"I Know My Sin Was Great, But the Penalty Is Great Too."

Martha Jule Beck was too large to fit into the electric chair at Sing Sing. She squirmed, twisted, and finally settled between the two fixed arms of the chair which, on that same evening of March 8, 1951, had already executed three men. The first two were both 22-year-olds who had senselessly killed a radio technician during a robbery. The third to go was Raymond Fernandez, her partner in crime. Martha was saved for last because it was tradition to save the strongest for last. All four were executed between 11:02 and 11:24 p.m.— a fast pace by any standard.

Martha was not without nicknames—variously referred to as the "Obese Ogress," "Overweight Juliet," "Ray's Three-Hundred-Pound Lovey-Dovey." She and Fernandez were convicted of killing an elderly widow in New York. There were other homicides (some suggest as many as 17). They were arrested in Michigan for killing Mrs. Delphine Downing and her 20-month-old daughter. Downing was shot in a scuffle and Rainelle, the daughter, was drowned later when she wouldn't stop crying. Since Michigan had no death penalty at that time and New York did, an agreement was reached by Governor Thomas Dewey of New York and Governor C. Mennen Williams of Michigan whereby the couple would be extradited to New York but, if not convicted, they could be returned to Michigan to stand trial there.

Both Beck and Fernandez came from abusive homes—her's in Florida, his in Spain. She was the youngest of five children and had been overweight from childhood. After claiming to have been raped twice by her brother and fearing she was pregnant, her mother gave her a secret family remedy and her period began again. She read romance novels and created fantasies to make her dull life seem more romantic. She had been married three times and had a daughter and a son. There probably would have been a fourth husband but, at hearing that she was pregnant he attempted suicide by jumping off a California wharf, leaving her to deal with the fact that he preferred death to marrying her.

Her employment history included working in a maternity home in Pensacola, Florida, and serving as the Superintendent of the Crippled Children's Home.

As for Fernandez, he read adventure and mystery novels to match his fantasies of power and heroism. He was married and left a wife and children in Spain. At one time he had served as mayor of the Spanish town of Orgiva. His life for the most part was fairly conventional. He was a good father and husband until "the accident." Fernandez was working onboard an oil tanker that had sailed from Gibraltar when he was hit on the head by a falling hatch. He was hit hard enough to cave in his skull and leave a scar on his brain tissue.

After this accident, Fernandez reported having headaches and being afflicted with, "strange and inexplicable sex drives."[42] To treat his headaches he would buy Benzedrex inhalers, divide the wick into pieces, and chew them. To treat his other problem he turned to prostitutes and lonely hearts club ads.

With this background it was no surprise that Beck and Fernandez found each other. They met through Mother Dinene's Friendly Club for Lonely Hearts. She responded to his ad, altering to some extent her actual description, and he answered in his typical dapper, enchanting, Charles Boyer manner. They met in Pensacola. She took it seriously; he referred to her as "the fat bitch." She thought they would marry; he sent her a letter on the day her friends were giving her a bridal shower, telling her he never felt anything for her. She turned on the gas jets to kill herself but was discovered by neighbors in time to save her. He found out about this attempt, apologized to her, she accepted and he was stuck with her. For his love she lost her job, abandoned her two children and participated in what, at their trial, was referred to as "perverted sex."

The two of them teamed up and continued his scheme of deceiving lonely women, promising to marry them, getting their money and then skipping town. They introduced themselves as brother and sister. What an unusual pair they made—he with his suave, Charles Boyer appearance and black toupee and she with her weight problem (over 300 pounds), perpetual halitosis, and double chins. After their arrest they were dubbed the "lonely hearts slayers." The press constantly had pejorative comments to make about Martha's appearance. At one time she retorted:

> "Am I being tried for murder or because I am fat? Maybe if a few people could have understood what it's like to be laughed at all your life because you're fat, I wouldn't be where I am now."[43]

Both were tried for the murder of a Mrs. Fay, whose friends became suspicious about her absence and sent the police to her home—where they found Beck and Fernandez and a freshly poured slab of cement in the basement. Mrs. Fay had been beaten in the head with a hammer and strangled. Her body was found under a slab of concrete in the basement of the home Beck and Fernandez had rented—just so they could dispose of the body.

Both confessed and Martha pled insanity on the basis of a claim to *folie a deux*—the idea that two sane people can inspire each other to do insane things through a sustained and prolonged relationship. The jury of 10 men and 2 women did not buy this defense and found them both guilty. The trial was attended by "a seething mass of struggling, shoving, semi-hysterical women," who were described mostly as "plump, middle-aged or elderly women seeking vicarious sex thrills from the spectacle of the two unglamourous lovers on trial for their lives."[44] The murderers were sentenced to death in Sing Sing's electric chair.

The death chamber at this time was referred to as the "little green room" and described as having walls of which the bottom half was painted dark green with black trim. The ceiling was cream-colored and the electric chair sat opposite the green entry door.

Martha and Fernandez awaited execution in Sing Sing's death house. Its construction was such that they were kept in separate areas but could see each other if a certain door was left open. They spent their time sending notes to each other proclaiming their undying love.

Their pending execution did not appear to dampen their appetites. Martha had liver and onions for lunch and Southern fried chicken for her last dinner. Fernandez ate a lunch of fried eggs and french fried potatoes followed by chocolate and a cigarette. His last dinner was an onion omelette (Spanish style) with almond ice cream and coffee for dessert.

At the time of their execution each uttered a final statement. Beck said:

What does it matter who is to blame? My story is a love story, but only those tortured with love can understand what I mean. I was pictured as a fat unfeeling woman. True. I am fat, that I cannot deny, but if that is a crime, how many of my sex are guilty? I am not unfeeling, stupid or moronic. The prison and the death house have only strengthened my feeling for Raymond, and in the history of the world how many crimes have been attributed to love? My last words are and my last thoughts will be: He who is without sin cast the first stone.[45]

The chaplain then asked her if she had repented and she replied:

I know my sin was great, but the penalty is great too. That makes things even, I guess.[46]

Fernandez simply stated:

I am going to die. That is all right. As you know that's something I've been prepared for since 1949. So tonight I'll die like a man.[47]

Headlines next morning from the *New York Daily News* reported:

HEARTS KILLERS
DIE IN CHAIR
MARTHA GOES WITH SMILE, WINK

Perhaps it was not love as much as the killing that bound Martha Jules Beck and Raymond Fernandez together. Fyodor Dostoyevsky, in *The Possessed*, conveyed it best:

Can you count on your fingers the people who can be accepted as members of your circles? All this is just bureaucracy and sentimentality—all this is just so much cement, but there's one thing that is much better—persuade four [or two] members of the circle to murder a fifth [or a third?] . . . and you'll at once tie them in a knot by the blood shed. They'll be your slaves.[48]

New York was not, of course, the only state to execute women by electrocution—just the first. Eleven states have executed a total of 25 women by electrocution. New York has executed the most, with Alabama, four, and Ohio with three. Alabama, for a while, used a portable electric chair. It was constructed in a trailer and could be pulled from county to county and hooked up to a local power source.

ALABAMA

Selina Gilmore—"I'm Going Home Where the Angels Dwell."

Selina Gilmore, a black woman, died in the electric chair at Kilby Prison in Montgomery, Alabama. She was executed for the death of a waiter who had asked her to leave the restaurant. She had entered drunk and disorderly. She left after he asked her to, but she returned with a gun and shot him to death. Selina became the first woman to die in Alabama's electric chair. She was executed on January 24, 1930. Present at the execution was the uncle of the slain waiter, who described her last moments as follows:

"Jesus Loves Me Because I First Loved Him" she sang in her cell as I stood against the rail just before the chair. Then I heard the clank of the jailer's keys and I heard the lock turn. And then Selina Gilmore walked in to the room. She had a towel tied about her head. She walked in strong, and without asking mercy, or saying anything, she sat in the chair, and the men began to strap her down. She and the preacher were singing. They were singing, "I'm Going Home Where The Angels Dwell."

When the towel was pulled off, I saw her head had been shaved. Then the warden asked her if she had anything to say . . . She said corn whiskey had made her do it. . .They tightened the throat strap . . . and dropped a black rag over her face, and a minute later there was a great whirring sound. The straps were creaking and groaning as her body strained outward against them. The little blue coil of smoke twisted upward from her head. All of a sudden the current stopped. She collapsed just like a wet towel. She sank back in the chair.

The doctors straightened out her fingers and started to test her heart when Selina Gilmore moved her head. Twice it wagged . . . Her chest rose and fell—once she breathed. It was a great puff of wind bursting out from tortured lungs. Quickly the lever was thrown and there she was, once more rigid, once more the straps creaking and groaning, and once more the blue coil of smoke. The smell in the tiny room was all of singed flesh. One man clapped his hands over his mouth and ran for fresh air.

And then once more she collapsed. The doctors looked at her fingernails, examined her heart. They said she was dead. When they said that I felt a great relief.[49]

Two of the other women executed in Alabama were both poisoners.

Earle Dennison—"God Has Forgiven Me For All I Have Done."

Earle Dennison died for poisoning her 2-year-old niece. She was the first white woman to be executed in Alabama. Evidence suggested she had also poisoned another niece 2 years earlier, but she was not tried for that death. She was tried and found guilty of poisoning Shirley Diann Weldon. She had given the 2-year-old child a drink of orange pop containing arsenic as the child sat on her lap and hugged her. She then left the dying child lying in bed as she hurried off to make a late payment on the child's life insurance policy. Earle Dennison tried twice to take her own life while awaiting execution. Her last meal consisted of fried chicken, green salad, mashed potatoes and coffee. She was executed on September 4, 1953. Her last words were, "God has forgiven me for all I have done. I have forgiven everybody and I hope everybody has forgiven me."[50]

Rhonda Belle Martin—"I Want My Body to Be Given to Some Scientific Institution. . . ."

Rhonda Belle Martin died on October 11, 1957, in the same electric chair as both Selina Gilmore and Earle Dennison, at Kilby Prison. According to news reports she "liked to take care of people." Over a period of 20 years she killed six people by poisoning them—including two of her five husbands, three of her children, and her mother. She was arrested after an attempt to poison her fifth husband failed and he was left paralyzed. He was the son of one of her previous husbands, a victim of her rat poison.

Her last meal consisted of hamburger, mashed potatoes, cinnamon rolls, and coffee. She was repeating the 23rd Psalm as she entered the death chamber. It took 6 minutes to strap her into the chair and 8 minutes later she was pronounced dead. She left a note in her cell requesting:

At my death, whether it be a natural death or otherwise, I want my body to be given to some scientific institution to be used as they see fit, but especially to see if someone can find out why I committed the crimes I have committed. I can't understand it, for I had no reason whatsoever. There is definitely something wrong. Can't someone find it and save someone else the agony I have been through?[51]

Ohio has executed three women in the electric chair.

OHIO

Anna Marie Hahn—"[D]on't Do This to Me. . .Can't You Think of My Baby?"

Anna Marie Hahn died on December 7, 1938. She was a German immigrant school teacher who became the first woman to die in Ohio's electric chair. Like those in Alabama, she was a poisoner—perhaps the original "Black Widow." She befriended elderly German gentlemen—five of them at least, possibly as many as 15—who died mysterious deaths, each leaving her and her young son a little better off financially. It is not known exactly how many men she poisoned. Although some evidence suggests she might also have poisoned her first husband, who died from an unknown illness. Referred to variously as "Ohio's Borgia," the "Black Widow," and the "Beautiful Blonde Killer," Anna stole prescription blanks from her doctor and, after filling them out for poison crystals, would send her young son to the pharmacy to obtain them. She then fed the poison to elderly men whom she then pretended to nurse back to health while watching them die a slow death.

Her jury consisted of 11 housewives and 1 man. She was found guilty and sentenced to die in the electric chair. Her hopes for clemency were dashed when Governor Martin L. Davey refused to stop her execution:

I have always regarded the power of pardon and commutation vested in the governor, as an emergency power, to be used with great discretion and in a judicial manner, or to correct inequality of punishment or to correct some error that may have occurred in the application of the law.

In thinking this case through, and in the midst of every effort to find a reason to commute her sentence to life, one opposing thought always surged forward. What could I say to the mothers whose sons committed only one murder, and then perhaps not quite as cold and calculating as the several murders committed by Mrs. Hahn? There is no way to measure the anguish of a mother's heart, who sees her wayward son, her own flesh and blood, go to the chair. The love of a mother for her child is infinitely greater than the affection which a boy can feel for a mother who has to go.[52]

Anna's 12-year-old son, Oscar, visited her almost every day while she was on death row. He appealed to the governor through newspapers and in person for her life. When reporters asked him what he would say to the governor, he responded, "I want to ask him if there isn't anything he can do for my mother. I want to tell him that she's the best mother in the world and that I know she didn't do these things they say she did."[53]

On December 7, 1938, Anna Marie Hahn, dressed in blue cotton pajamas and a brown silk robe, walked the 150 feet, past 11 men awaiting their own deaths, to the death chamber. The trip took her 5 minutes. As she entered the chamber and saw the electric chair, she cried to the warden, "[D]on't do this to me. Think of my boy. Can't you think of my baby?" Turning to the assembled witnesses she pled, "Isn't there anybody who will help me? Is nobody going to help me?"[54]

One of the matrons who spent the last days with Anna Hahn and stayed with her during her execution summed up her impressions: "I do feel that in spite of her vanity, her conceit, her stubbornness, her guilt, some of the good things should be remembered about her—she was so human, so human."[55]

Actor George Raft invited Oscar to go to his home in Hollywood, all expenses paid. He wanted to help the boy get over his mother's execution and to be able to think of something else during the Christmas holidays. I don't know if Oscar accepted the invitation or not.

The execution of Anna Marie Hahn cost the State of Ohio $10,000. It would be another 16 years before the next execution in Ohio. The first of these was also a poisoner, Blanche "Dovie" Dean.

Blanche Dean—"[He] Wanted a Housekeeper and I Wanted a Home."

Blanche "Dovie" Dean finally confessed to poisoning her 69-year-old husband, Hawkins Dean, by putting rat poison in his milk. She tried to frame her son by a previous marriage but eventually confessed when the sheriff commented that "any woman who could accuse her son of such a crime could easily have done it herself."[56] She said the killing took place after several violent arguments when she found her new husband (her third) could not "perform his husbandly duties." Dovie, the mother of five children, grandmother of eight, was quickly dubbed the "Grandmother Slayer" and the "Woman Who Can't Cry." After her trial she commented:

When I got on the witness stand they made light of me because I couldn't cry. Years ago, I couldn't have faced all of those people, but I asked God to help me. . . . I had grief inside, like knives.[57]

The grief she referred to included the broken home she came from; her early marriage to a man who went to prison for assaulting her daughter, eventually resulting in the daughter's death; the death of her son in a boiler explosion; and her marriage to Hawkins Dean. Of him, she said, "[H]e wanted a housekeeper and I wanted a home."

Dovie's last meal consisted of roast chicken, potatoes, asparagus, green salad with French dressing, coconut cream pie, angel food cake, and coffee. She invited news reporters to join her. "Won't you have a bite of this roast chicken? I have so much I don't know if I can finish it."[58] All declined. The steward serving her later commented, "Sitting there with her hands folded in her lap, she looked just like Whistler's Mother."[59]

Dovie Dean, age 55, the "Woman Who Can't Cry," entered the death chamber on January 15, 1954, at 8:00 p.m. wearing a "simple green dress buttoned down the front, white anklets and brown shoes."[60] She had been baptized a Methodist a few days earlier and was accompanied by three clergy, two Protestant ministers and the Catholic chaplain of the prison. She was pronounced dead 7 minutes later. According to those who had witnessed executions before, "they had never seen a condemned prisoner meet final fate more placidly."[61] To the end, she could not, or would not, cry.

Betty Butler—"My Work Is Done."

Betty Butler died in the same electric chair almost 6 months later to the day. She became the third woman to be executed in Ohio's electric chair, the first black woman and, to date, the last woman to die in Ohio.

Betty Butler was sentenced to die for the strangulation and drowning of Evely Clark at Sharon Woods Lake. They had been fishing in a boat with a male companion when an argument started. He put them ashore where the argument continued. Betty then strangled Evely until she was unconscious and dragged her to the edge of the lake and pushed her in until her head and shoulders were under water. Witnesses said she then shouted, "My work is done!" Butler claimed her actions were self-defense, in that Clark had made her a "sex slave" and she killed her to escape her "perverted intentions." She was found guilty and sentenced to die. She became known as the "Sphinx of the Reformatory," being "polite but never friendly" to those around her. She was visited before her execution by her husband, Henry, as well as by Quo Vadis her 5-year-old daughter, Donnie, her 6-year-old son, and her mother. Her last meal consisted of a bowl of apricots, milk, toast and scrambled eggs with cheese. She was originally sentenced to die the same day as Dovie Dean but stays of execution postponed the date for 6 months. She entered the death chamber on June 12, 1954, dressed in a pink-and-black print dress, white oxfords, and bobby socks. She was accompanied by a Catholic priest from whom she had been taking instructions in the Catholic faith. Carrying a rosary she sat in the chair with only a quiet murmur. At 8:10 p.m., the 26-year-old mother of two was pronounced dead.

Two other states have executed two women in the electric chair—Pennsylvania and South Carolina.

PENNSYLVANIA

Irene Schroeder—"I Am Going to Die. . .But I Am Not Afraid."

On February 23, 1931, Pennsylvania executed the "Trigger Woman." Irene Schroeder was sentenced to die for her participation in a grocery store robbery which ended in a shoot-out and the death of a highway patrolman. She and two male companions (with her 4-year-old son Donnie also in the car) were escaping the scene of the robbery when they were stopped by the patrolman and another officer. Both officers were shot, one fatally.

In their search for Irene, the police questioned her son, who was staying with relatives. During the questioning he said, "My mama shot one cop and he laid back off the car groaning. Uncle Tom shot another one in the head. He shot right through the windshield."[62] Police began a search for Irene Schroeder, her brother Tom (T.D.) Crawford, and Walter Glenn Dague. Crawford was never caught. It was believed he was killed in a shoot-out after a Texas bank robbery. Dague and Irene ("Iron Irene," the "Blonde Bandit") were later arrested in Arizona after a shoot-out that killed yet another officer. Brought back to Pennsylvania, both were found guilty and sentenced to die— Irene to become the first woman executed by electrocution in Pennsylvania. She died at 7:05 a.m. She wore "a gray dress of imitation silk with white collar and cuffs, beige silk stockings and black satin slippers."[63] Her executioner, Robert Elliot, described her as the "most composed and fearless person I have ever put to death."[64] As he left his mother for the last time, son Donnie said, "I'll bet Mom would make an awful nice angel."[65] Irene's last words for her father were, "You did all you could, pop, I'm ready to die." To her son she said, "I am going to die, my boy, but I am not afraid. Be a good boy and don't be afraid."[66]

Corrine Sykes

Irene was followed 15 years later by Corrine Sykes. The 20-year-old black housemaid was sentenced to die for stabbing and robbing the woman she worked for in Philadelphia. Her male accomplice was sentenced as an accessory. Sykes was the youngest woman to ever receive a death sentence in Pennsylvania. Her defense claimed she had the mentality of an 8-year-old and was easily led. The prosecution claimed the butcher knife killing was "an extremely cruel, cold-blooded and atrocious murder."[67] For her last meal, Sykes had "a special menu . . . prepared in the superintendent's private home."[68] She died on October 14, 1946, at 12:31 a.m., after leaving only a letter for her mother.

South Carolina also executed two women in the electric chair.

SOUTH CAROLINA

Sue Logue—"I Am Ready to Go."

Sue Logue began her route to execution when her mule kicked to death a calf belonging to the neighbor. In the argument that ensued, her husband was killed. He was only the first of eight people who would eventually die over the incident, including three who would die in the electric chair. Eventually the neighbor who killed Logue's husband was tried and acquitted. Later he would be killed as would the sheriff and his deputy who came to serve papers on Sue Logue. A sharecropper who was defending Logue with a shotgun also died in the shoot-out. Sue Logue and two accomplices were executed, one after the other, on January 15, 1943. She became the first woman executed in the electric chair in South Carolina, the third in the state's history.

Rose Marie Stinette—"Root Doctor"

Four years later, Rose Marie Stinette became the second woman to die in the same electric chair. A black woman, she had a face and a body whose left side was almost totally scarred. At the age of 49, she looked more like 60. She had a reputation as a local "Root Doctor" and, along with three others, was indicted for the murder of her husband. It was discovered that she had eight insurance policies on her husband's life. Of the four black people arrested, Stinette and one of those she hired to do the killing were sentenced to die. The other two, including her boyfriend, were given life sentences. After a last minute commutation of her codefendant by Governor Williams (who was serving his last few days in office and had granted several pardons and commutations), Stinette became the only person executed for the crime. She attempted to get a temporary stay by claiming she was pregnant but an X ray proved this false. She died on January 17, 1947. As the switch was thrown, a short circuit blew a fuse. "Witnesses then saw sparks from the woman's head and arms dimly illuminate the death scene, before somebody struck a match to provide more light."[69]

Stinette became the first "Negress" executed in the electric chair, the second woman in the state's history.

The states that have executed only one woman in their electric chairs include Virginia, Illinois, Louisiana, Mississippi, and Georgia.

VIRGINIA

Virginia Christian—"I'm Right Much Worried."

Virginia Christian, a 17-year-old black girl, died on August 16, 1912. She died quietly in what was referred to by the press as the "Chamber of Quick Retribution." She was executed for the robbery and murder of her white employer, Ida Belote. Mrs. Belote had been beaten and strangled. A broom handle was then used to force her tongue, a towel, and some of her hair down her throat. The newspaper quoted Virginia's confession as follows:

> She [Mrs. Belote] come to mammer's house dat morning an' say she want me to come an' do some washin'. When I come home mommer say Miss Belote want me an' I went 'roun' to de house. I wen' in de back way an' when she see me she asked me about a gold locket she missed. I told her I ain't seen it an' don't know nuthin' about it. She also say sumthin' about a skirt but de main thing was the locket. She say "yes you got it an' if you don't bring it back, I'm goin' to have you put in jail."

> I got mad an' told her if I did have it, she wasn't goin' to git it back. Den she picked up de spittoon and hit me wit it an' it broke. They wuz two sticks in de room, broom handles. She run for one, an' I for de' other. I got my stick fust an' I hit her wit it 'side de hade and she fell down. She kep' hollerin' so I took a towel and stuffed it in her mouth. I helt it there twel she quit hollerin' and jes' groaned. I didn't mean to kill her an' I didn't know I had. I was mad when I hit her an' stuffed the towel in her mouth to keep her from hollerin'. I never meant to kill her. When I lef' she was groanin' and layin' on her back.[70]

After the murder, it was reported that Virginia washed her hands, took the valuables, and left the house. She was arrested, tried, found guilty and sentenced to die. The newspaper described her situation as follows:

Notwithstanding her confession to her spiritual adviser and to others that she killed Mrs. Ida Belote, and notwithstanding a clean bath and good breakfast, Virginia Christian was a doleful little nigger gal, when seen in her cell in the Hampton jail this morning and "wasn't feeling so mighty good." She had not slept very well and even when slumber came at fitful intervals, she had been haunted in her dreams by the ghost of the woman she slew. Her condition this morning was pitiful.[71]

In her cell, awaiting execution, she claimed the ghost of her victim haunted her in her dreams. The ghost of Mrs. Belote would appear and write on the wall "De reason I'm daid is because I made Virg mad."

Virginia was described as:

[A] full-blooded negress, with kinky hair done up with threads, with dark lusterless eyes and with splotches on the skin of her face. Her color is dark brown, and her figure is short, dumpy and squashy. She has had some schooling, but her speech does not betray it. Her language is the same as the unlettered members of her race. Her intelligence is below average, and her moral standard is evidently very low.[72]

Before her execution Virginia made a confession. "I know that I am getting no more than I deserve. I am prepared to answer for my sins, and I believe that the Lord has forgiven me. I fear that Mrs. Belote may not have been a Christian . . . I hope to meet Mrs. Belote in Heaven."[73]

ILLINOIS

Marie Porter—"I Hold No Malice Towards Anyone."

On the morning of his wedding, William Kappan was abducted by one woman and two men. The woman was his sister, Marie Porter, who had hired John and Angelo Gianeola, brothers, to help her. Mrs. Porter demanded that Kappen not change his insurance policy. She had been listed as the beneficiary of the $3,300 policy but now that her brother was marrying, he told her his new wife was to become the beneficiary. He refused to make any changes and was consequently shot in the head by one of her accomplices. The body was then dragged into a field on the side of the road. Unfortunately for the killers, the field was full of poison ivy and it was easy to later trace the trio. John Gianeola quickly confessed and implicated the other two. He received 99 years in prison. His brother Angelo and Marie Porter were sentenced to die.

Governor Henry Horner refused to grant executive clemency, but during his absence from the state, the lieutenant governor did grant a week's reprieve. At his return, the governor again refused to commute Mrs. Porter's sentence although he had done so for the previous three women sentenced to die during his tenure in office. Marie Porter, mother of four daughters, mastermind behind the killing, died in the Illinois electric chair on January 28, 1938.

Marie was only the second woman executed in Illinois. The first was Elizabeth Reed who was hanged in 1845 for poisoning her husband. It is reported she "went to the gallows singing hymns and riding on her own casket."

LOUISIANA

Toni Jo Henry—"The Victim Doesn't Return to Haunt Me. I Never Think of Him."

Toni Jo Henry loved her husband, Claude "Cowboy" Henry. The problem was he was in a Texas prison. Posing as hitchhikers, Toni Jo (prostitute and drug addict) and a man called Arkansas (Harold Burks, an ex-con and army deserter) flagged down a car. Once in the car they killed the driver shortly after crossing from Texas into Louisiana. His body was left covered with straw in a rice field. The sole purpose was to steal a car so Toni Jo could break Cowboy out of prison. Arkansas, after the killing, traveled with Toni Jo to a hotel where Toni Jo hit him over the head, abandoned him unconscious and left on a bus–since she couldn't drive. Both were arrested and sentenced to die. She was executed November 28, 1942; he was executed in March of 1943—both by the state of Louisiana.

Born Annie Beatrice McQuiston, she changed her name at the age of 14 to Toni Jo. She met Cowboy Henry in a house of prostitution where they fell in love. Cowboy was awaiting a second trial for killing a former police officer in San Antonio. He was subsequently found guilty and sentenced to 50 years in prison. As the sentence was given, Toni Jo ran to his side crying, "I'll get you out, Cowboy, don't worry."

While she awaited her execution on Louisiana's death row, Cowboy Henry escaped twice from prison in his attempt to reach her and break her out. Each time he was recaptured before making any contact. Just before her execution, both of them were allowed to talk to each other by telephone—she in Louisiana, he in Texas.

Later, at receiving news of her execution, he is reported to have "cried like a baby" and spent time in his solitary confinement cell "gibbering and weeping." Toni Jo's last words to him were for him to "live an upright and law-abiding life, and to 'go out' the front door instead of the back." She also told him to "behave like a man and make his mother proud."

MISSISSIPPI

Mildred Johnson

Mildred Louise Johnson died in Mississippi's portable electric chair on May 19, 1944, for the murder of Annie Laurie Conklin. Miss "Nannie," as Conklin was known to her friends, was a 74-year-old woman who lived alone. She was bent and crippled and used a cut-off broom handle to assist her when she walked. Her badly beaten body was discovered in her home.

Mildred Johnson was arrested a few days later when she left her purse in a taxi after she couldn't pay the $1.50 cab fare. The driver took the purse into a restaurant and gave it to the police. When they looked inside they found it belonged to Mildred but that it also contained receipts and ration books belonging to Annie Conklin. Both Johnson (alias James) and Conklin were black.

Mildred confessed to the killing and implicated two men as accomplices. They were both tried, but acquitted. Mildred Johnson was sentenced to die. At her request, the straps of the portable electric chair were adjusted for comfort. She was pronounced dead at 4:16 a.m.

GEORGIA

Lena Baker

Claiming self-defense and that she had been forced to be his "slave woman," Lena Baker, a black woman, was sentenced to die for killing E.B. Knight, a white operator of a grist mill. The mother of three children, Baker said Knight threatened her with an iron bar and she shot him to protect herself. She was executed on March 5, 1945. [For the rest of the story, see the update for the 21st Century.]

COMPARISON CASES: EFFIE JOWERS—"HAMMER SLAYER" AND NANNIE HAZEL DOSS—"ARSENIC ANNIE"

It almost seems to have been contagious. Their husbands (or wives) were in the way of a new relationship. The easiest thing to do was to eliminate the problem. Ruth Snyder and Judd Gray killed Ruth's husband, Ada LeBoeuf and Doc Dreher killed Ada's husband, and Mary Creighton and Everett Applegate killed Applegate's wife. All six were executed. But there were cases similar (almost identical) in which the offenders were not executed. They occurred during the same time period, with people approximately the same age and for nearly the same motives.

The body of J. F. (Frank) Jowers, age 55, was found in Caney Creek. It was under a small bridge where it had been weighted down with 100 pounds of scrap iron—a flatiron tied to the feet, two iron wheels around the stomach, and a strap around the neck—which held the body staked to the shore 18 inches beneath the water's surface.

Community gossip which linked Jowers' wife Effie, age 38, and J.E. (Elisha) Swift, age 48, resulted in their arrest. Subsequent confessions of the two indicated that Effie Jowers, mother of five children, held a lantern (à la LeBoeuf) as Swift (her paramour) killed her sleeping husband (à la Snyder). He was killed on Halloween night—October 31, 1927. Swift waited in a closet for Jowers to go to sleep. Jowers also carried a $2,000 insurance policy.

A few months before his death, Jowers had visited the local sheriff complaining about Swift's attentions to his wife and of Swift's negative influence on the Jowers' 13-year-old son, who had recently been arrested with Swift on a liquor charge. The sheriff advised Mr. Jowers if things at home were so bad he should "arrange his affairs and leave home."

"If I had heard that Jowers had disappeared, I would have thought that he was taking my advice," the sheriff later said.

Suspicion was aroused when Mrs. Jowers was observed varnishing her bedroom floor. Later, investigators turned up blood between the cracks of the floor. Swift's 16-year-old son led deputies to the creek where he had been forced to help dispose of the body or face a "flogging" from his father.

Effie Jowers and James Elisha Swift offered to plead guilty if they could escape the death penalty, but their offer was refused.

After an in-depth sanity hearing, both were found sane and capable of standing trial. It was, however, discovered during that hearing that Elisha Swift's father had once been indicted for murder. After twice being tried and finally acquitted, and after his wife's suicide while he was in jail, Elisha's father returned home and placed his five children (four daughters and Elisha) with various families in the community. He then left the state and was never heard from again.

The defense won the right to another sanity hearing—this time before the court. While this hearing was going on, arrangements were suddenly made for Jowers and Swift to plead guilty "without capital punishment." The judge accepted their pleas and they were immediately sentenced to life in prison.

Four of these women who died in the electric chair were poisoners. Other women poisoners have been executed by other means as well. Some authors have suggested poison is a woman's weapon and, historically, this would seem to be the case.

In an article on arsenic poisoning, Michael S. Gorby traces part of the historical background of arsenic as a weapon.[74] He suggests arsenic, because of the uses to which it has been put, has the "worst public relations record of any element." He adds that "The poisoner became an integral part of social and political life in the early Middle Ages. . . ."[75] Arsenic became so popular and was used to such an extent that it acquired the name *poudre de succession*, or "inheritance powder."

Gorby indicates arsenic was used by the infamous Borgias and soon became the favorite poison of nineteenth century France:

> A French woman named Catherine Deshayes commercialized this service, which grew to infamous proportions, earning her the title, "La Vooine" [the neighbor]. Her business dissolved with her execution when a special judicial commission established by Louis XIV convicted her of many poisonings, including more than 2,000 infant victims.[76]

The use and popularity of arsenic was probably due less to its effectiveness and probably more to "its availability, inexpensiveness, and the fact that it is tasteless and odorless. . . ."[77] These very factors contribute to its popularity among women poisoners and, because arsenic deaths are often not recognized, led to the passage of Oklahoma's "Nannie Doss Law." This law required that a medical examination be conducted for any death that occurred without the physician being present. Who was Nannie Doss?

Forty-nine-year-old, Alabama native Nannie Hazel Doss was described by the prosecution as:

> [A] shrewd, clever, sharp, calculating, selfish, self-aggrandizing female whose aggressive behavior under frustration releases her hostility toward men—particularly her husbands. . . .[78]

She was described by one of the psychiatrists who examined her as insane and suffering from "states of elated giggling and depressive despondency."[79] Another psychiatrist defined her as narcissistic (a lover of self), functioning at a 5 or 6-year-old level and as "one of the cleverest criminals I've ever examined—and that covers 20 years of practice."[80]

The press gave her nicknames of "Arsenic Annie," "Merry Widow," "Lady Bluebeard," "Grandma Nannie," and my favorite, "The Giggling Grandma." They depicted her as a frizzy-haired, plump (sometimes rotund) defendant who appeared at the opening day of her sanity trial wearing "a green and white plaid cotton dress and chewing gum vigorously."[81] Her cellmate, Cleo Epps, known as the "Queen of the Bootleggers," described Nanny as "very nice."

Nannie Hazel Doss was arrested in Oklahoma in October of 1954 and charged with the death of her fifth husband, 58-year-old Samuel Doss. She was charged with putting rat poison in his prunes. In her confession she stated, "He sure did like prunes. . . .I fixed him a whole box and he ate them all."[82]

Although she was only charged with the death of Sam Doss, she eventually confessed to killing four husbands plus her mother. The list of suspected deaths, however, eventually reached 12—all by poisoning. These include the deaths of:

- Zelma and Gertrude—1½ and 2½, respectively, two of her children.
- Frank Harrelson—second husband.
- Robert Lee Higgins—2½-year-old grandson.
- Mrs. Dovie Weaver—sister.
- Arlie J. Laning—third husband.
- Unnamed—nephew of Arlie Laning.
- Mrs. Sue Hazel—mother.
- Mrs. Sula Bartee—sister.
- Jim Hazel—father.
- Richard L. Morton—fourth husband (and his dog).
- Samuel Doss—fifth husband.[83]

It was also discovered that, while Sam Doss lay dying, Nannie was corresponding with a potential sixth husband.

At her first trial—a sanity hearing—it was brought out that she still bore scars from when her father used to beat her with a chain. She married early—at the age of 15—and during her life she had continuously read romance and true detective stories. She joined lonely hearts clubs and corresponded with lonely men in an effort to find her "dream man."

Her motive for killing Sam Doss was that he got on her nerves with "little things":

[H]e refused to allow a radio in the home; wouldn't let her visit neighbors to watch television; wouldn't let her use a fan in summer to keep cool; and made her go to bed each night, when he did, at nightfall. "He said he had been a Christian man all his life, and that I would be a Christian woman."[84]

A 10-man, 2-woman jury found her sane and capable of standing trial, whereupon she pled guilty to killing Samuel Doss. She was never charged nor tried for any of the other murders, all of which occurred in states other than Oklahoma.

Although Nannie was eligible for the death penalty, District Judge Elmer Adams sentenced her to life in prison. He explained:

> The court believes that the people and legislature of our Christian and enlightened state have never contemplated the assessment of a death penalty against a mental defective in such a case as this.[85]

Among other reasons, he also stated:

> This court has never heard of a woman being put to death for any crime in Oklahoma. It may happen some day, but it would be a poor precedent, and the people of this state would very reluctantly see such come to pass.[86]
> [The 21st Century began with the executions of three women from Oklahoma during the first ten years.]

Interviewed in prison, in 1957, while serving her life sentence, she commented, "I wish the authorities would let me be tried in Kansas or North Carolina. Maybe they would give me the electric chair."[87] She further commented:

> When they get short [of help] in the kitchen I always offer to help out . . . but they have never let me work there.[88]

Nannie Hazel Doss died in prison of leukemia on June 2, 1965 — 10 years to the day after she entered prison.

Why are some women executed and others not?

NOTES

1. Elliot, Robert G. 1940. *Agent Of Death: The Memoirs Of An Executioner*. New York: E. P. Dutton & Co., Inc., p.188.
2. Ibid., p.191. *Agent Of Death*.
3. Lawes, Lewis E. 1932. *Twenty Thousand Years In Sing Sing*. New York: Ray Long & Richard R. Smith, Inc., pp. 311–312.
4. Ibid., p.316.
5. *Ogden Standard Examiner*, January 10, 1985, p.1.
6. Drimmer, Frederick. 1990. *Until You Are Dead: The Book of Executions in America*. New York: Carol Publishing Group, p.21.
7. *New York Times*, March 21, 1899, p.3.
8. *New York Times*, March 16, 1899, p.1.
9. *New York Times*, March 24, 1909.

10. *New York Times*, March 30, 1909, p.1.

11. Ibid., p.6.

12. Ibid.

13. *New York Times*, January 3, 1928, p.14.

14. *New York Times*, January 14, 1928, p.8.

15. *New York Times*, January 13, 1928, p.1.

16. Bauman, Ed. 1993. *May God Have Mercy On Your Soul*. Chicago, Ill: Bonus Books, Inc., p.195–196.

17. Ibid., p.199.

18. *New York Times*, January 13, 1928, p.1.

19. Elliot, op.cit., p.187.

20. Ibid., p.190.

21. Lawes, op. cit., p.313.

22. *Ogden Standard Examiner*, August 10, 1934.

23. Brown, Wenzel. 1958. *Women Who Died In The Chair: The Dramatic True Stories Of Six Women Who Committed The Deadliest Sin*. New York: Collier Books, p.144.

24. Ibid., p.63–65.

25. Elliot, op.cit., p.214.

26. *New York Times*, Aug. 10,1934, p.1.

27. Kilgallin, Dorothy. 1967. *Murder One*. New York: Random House, p.108.

28. Ibid., p.105.

29. *New York Times*, August 17, 1934.

30. This quote was found in a copy of Old Oneonta, by Edwin R. Moore, Volume 4. Published by the Upper Susquehanna Historical Society, 1965, p.1.

31. Kilgallin, op.cit., p.108.

32. Brown, op.cit., p.72.

33. *Newsweek*, November 24, 1934, p.19.

34. *New York Herald Tribune*, June 28, 1935.

35. Nash, Robert. 1981. *Look For The Woman*. New York: M. Evans and Co., p.95.

36. *Toronto Globe*, June 28, 1935, p.1.

37. Brown (1958), op.cit., pp.85–86.

38. Brown (1958), op.cit., p.86.

39. *Ogden Standard Examiner*, July 13, 1936, p.1.

40. Brown (1958), op.cit., p.144.

41. Brown (1958), p.141.

42. Brown, Wenzell. 1952. *The Lonely Hearts Murders*. New York: Greenberg Pub., p.48.

43. Brown (1958), op.cit.,p.165.

44. Brown (1952), op.cit., p.103.

45. Ibid., p.115.

46. Ibid.

47. Ibid., p.116.

48. Wilkinson, Paul. 1979. *Terrorism And The Liberal State*. New York: New York University Press, p. 101.

49. This is quoted directly from a newspaper whose source I have not been able to identify. The headline reads, "Uncle of Slain Restaurant Waiter Watches Negro Woman Burn For It." The uncle is identified as B.B. Johnson.

50. *The Alabama Journal*, September 4, 1953.

51. *The Alabama Journal*, October 11, 1957.

52. *Cincinnati Enquirer*, December 7, 1938.

53. Ibid.

54. *Salt Lake Tribune*, December 12, 1938, p.1.

55. *The Columbus Evening Dispatch*, December 8, 1938, p.8-B.

56. *Cincinnati Enquirer*, September 13, 1952, p.1.

57. Ibid.

58. Ibid.

59. Ibid.

60. *Columbus Evening Dispatch*, January 16, 1954, p.1.

61. Ibid.

62. *New York Times*, January 1, 1930, p.18.

63. *New York Times*, February 24, 1931, p.5.

64. Elliot, op.cit., p.221.

65. *New York Times*, February 21, 1931, p.6.

66. Ibid.

67. *Philadelphia Enquirer*, October 14, 1946, p.1.

68. Ibid.

69. *The Florence Morning News*, January 18, 1947, p.1.

70. *Newport News Times-Herald*, April 11, 1912, p.1.

71. Ibid.

72. Ibid.

73. *Newport News Times-Herald*, April 16, 1912, p.1.

74. Gorby, Michael S. 1988. "Arsenic Poisoning." The Western Journal of Medicine, (September) 149:308–315.

75. Ibid., p.310.

76. Ibid.

77. Ibid.

78. *Tulsa Tribune*, May 2, 1955, p.1.

79. *Tulsa Tribune*, May 3, 1955, p.1.

80. Ibid.

81. *Tulsa Tribune*, May 2, 1955, p.1.

82. *Tulsa World*, November 29, 1954, p.1.

83. Ibid.

84. Ibid.

85. Tulsa Daily World, June 2, 1955, p.1.

86. Ibid.

87. Tulsa World's OK Magazine, October 22, 1978, p.9.

88. Ibid.

Velma Margie Barfield, North Carolina—Executed on November 2, 1984. She confessed to murdering four victims by poisoning with arsenic. (UPI/Corbiss-Bettmann)

Winnie Ruth Judd ("The Velvet Tigress"), Arizona—Not Executed, Death Sentence Commuted. Found guilty of the killings and dismembering of her two roommates. These pictures show her at the time of her arrest in Los Angeles on October 20, 1931. Her left hand is shown bandaged after a police surgeon removed a bullet that had been fired into her hand sometime during the commission of her crime. (UPI/Corbis-Bettmann)

Ruth Snyder ("The Granite Woman"), New York—Executed on January 12, 1929. Shown here in the electric chair. This is the famous "stolen" picture taken by Tom Howard in the death chamber at Sing Sing. Howard, a Chicagoan, unknown to New York prison authorities, used a 16mm one shot camera strapped to his ankle with the shutter release controlled from his pocket. (UPI/Corbis-Bettmann)

Lorraine Snyder, 11-Year-Old Daughter of Ruth Snyder. Shown praying for her mother who was executed in New York on January 12, 1929. P&A Photos (UPI/Corbis-Bettmann)

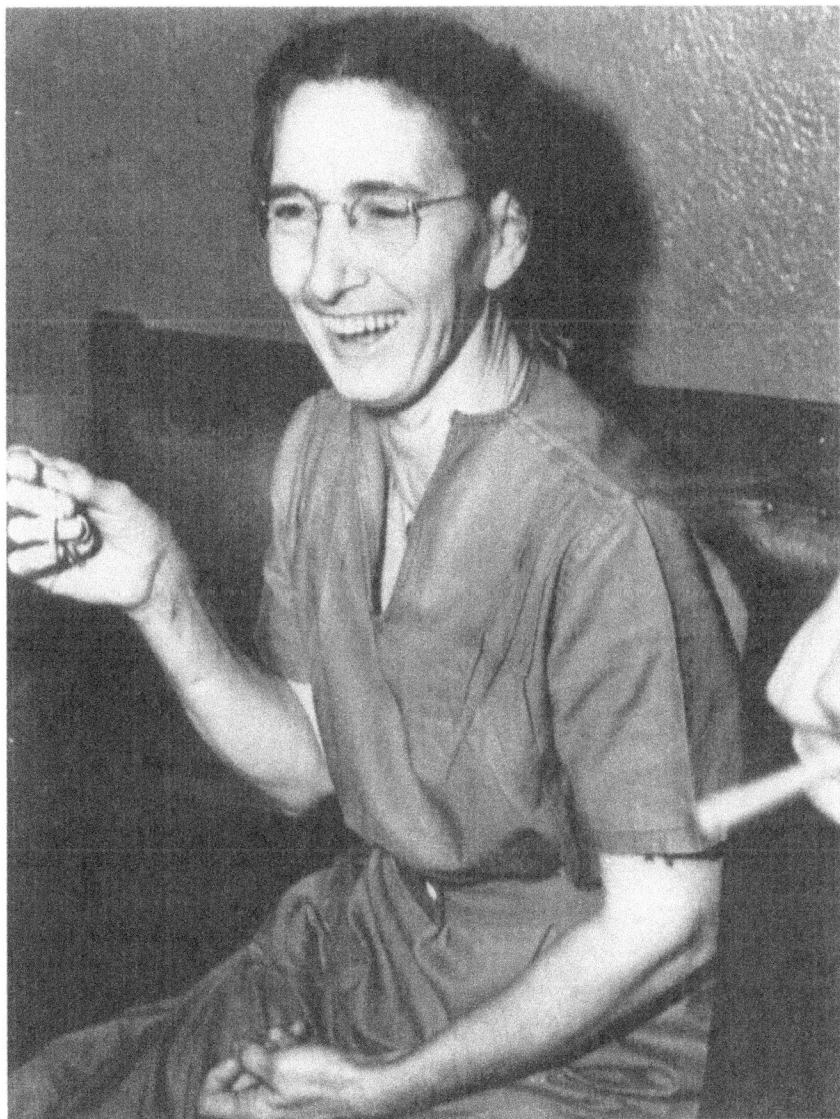

Juanita Spinelli ("The Duchess"), California—Executed on November 21, 1941. First woman executed in the gas chamber at San Quentin Prison. She had been convicted as head of a gang of thugs and murderers. (UPI/Corbis-Bettmann)

Martha Jule Beck ("Obese Ogress"), New York—Executed on March 8, 1951. Shown here arriving with her codefendant, Raymond Fernandez, at LaGuardia Airport, New York. Both "Lonely Hearts Slayers" were executed in the electric chair. (AP/Wide World Photos)

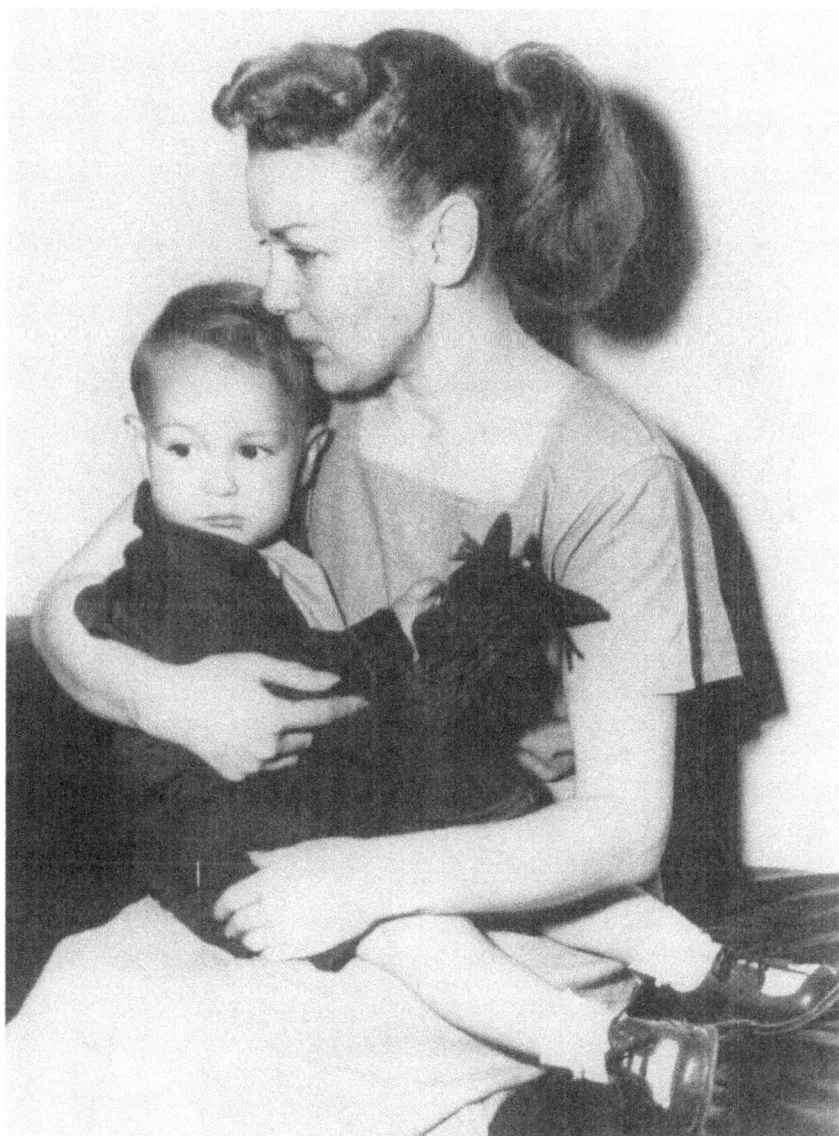

Barbara Graham ("Bloody Babs"), California—Executed on June 3, 1955. Shown here holding her 18-month-old son, Tommy, before her execution in California's gas chamber. She swore to her innocence on Tommy's head: "I hope my baby drops dead if I did it." (AP/World Wide Photos)

Elizabeth Duncan ("Ma"), California—Executed on August 8, 1962. Shown here with her son, Frank, whose pregnant wife she was convicted of hiring two men to kill. She and the two hired assassins were executed in the gas chamber at San Quentin. (AP/World Wide Photos)

Pictures of the dancehall ladies on the author's wall. (Jeff Bybee/Signpost)

Part Three

The Gas Chamber—"How in the Hell Would You Know?"

She had already been stopped twice on her way to the gas chamber. Once she was almost inside when the phone call came. This time the procession was halted again. "Why don't they stop torturing me?" she cried. Finally they were on their way in again. As she entered the room, apple green in color, Joe Ferreti, responsible for the execution, leaned over to her and said, "Barbara, after you hear the pellets drop into the acid, wait until the fumes are up around your nose, then take a deep breath and it won't hurt so much." With her head held high, showing off the features that made her an attractive prostitute, drug user, and dealer—a friend and companion to many men on the wrong side of the law—she looked him in the eye and retorted, "How in the hell would you know?" The question went unanswered as she was moved into the metallic capsule. The death chamber looked almost like a spaceship waiting for launch.

A few months ago I entered the apple green gas chamber at San Quentin. I walked up the approach to the main prison building. It reflected the architecture of the "big prison" days. I was taking the same route the women took at their arrival. I walked past the entrance to a small walkway into the gas chamber. After their long ride from Southern California Institution for Women, each of the four women who died here had to enter the room where the chamber stood. Men executed here entered from the other side, from the prison compound itself; they were kept at San Quentin.

As the women approached the door they could look up and see the T-shaped pipe used to vent the gas fumes from the chamber. But they could not see the chamber because it would have been covered with canvas to screen it from their view. It was necessary for them to follow this route to reach one of the two cells behind the execution room where they would spend the death-watch.

Only three states have used the gas chamber to execute women. Gas was first used as a form of execution by Nevada. There the move to use gas was introduced and the procedure proposed, with a rather interesting philosophy. An editorial in the *New York Times* stated:

> Not only has the Nevada Legislature refused to change its mind and the law as to the best, . . . most humane, way of putting condemned murderers to death, but it has complicated the state's "lethal chamber" method by ordaining that the deadly gas shall be administered while the condemned man is asleep.
>
>   This action will cause much comment, most of it, probably, adverse. There is something peculiarly dreadful in the voluntary, cold-blooded killing of a man by putting him in a tightly closed room and letting in on him a poisonous gas.[1]

The Nevada plan was intended to have pipes going into each of the death row cells and the gas could be introduced at any time. The condemned would never know when it was going to happen. For obvious reasons this procedure was found to be impractical and thus specific rooms or chambers were constructed and sealed.

Other states have used the gas chamber throughout its history, some with more success than others. In 1936, the wife of a man just executed in Arizona's gas chamber became ill after kissing her dead husband:

> Kisses pressed to the lips of her dead husband were blamed Friday for the serious illness of Mrs. Frank Rascon, wife of the Mexican cowboy executed for murder this morning. Frantic with grief, the woman threw herself upon her husband's body after the gas chamber was cleared of gas. Her kisses apparently contaminated her mouth with the deadly cyanide, which had killed Rascon, the sheriff's office said.[2]

California is the state that has executed the most women in the gas chamber.

CALIFORNIA

Juanita Spinelli—"My Blood Will Burn Holes in [Your] Bodies."

Ethel Leta Juanita Spinelli, age 52, became the first of four gas chamber executions. Her's was also California's first legal execution of a woman. The only other woman was another Juanita, "lynched" in Downieville in 1851. Warden Clinton Duffy, who was charged with the execution of the "Duchess," described her as "a homely, scrawny, nearsighted, sharp-featured, scarecrow, with thin lips, beady eyes, and scraggly black hair flecked with gray."[3] He said he was "amazed at her utter lack of feminine appeal." Governor C.L. Olson, to whom she appealed for mercy, commented:

> She is ignorant, frustrated and stupid. She has worked at menial tasks all her life, been knocked about by society, knowing only lowest criminal types among men. Her case presents a picture to make one wonder whether the state should treat such a case from the scientific or vengeful standpoint.[4]

Known as "The Duchess," she was head of a "gang" of "thugs and hoodlums" whom she trained to be criminals and masterminded their crimes. After a bungled robbery attempt that resulted in the death of a barbecue stand operator in San Francisco, she became concerned when one of the members of the gang seemed to weaken. Because there was fear he would go to the police, he was given knockout drops, dressed in a swim suit and thrown into the river, where he drowned. The Duchess, her daughter and three other gang members were arrested. Charges were not brought against her daughter, "The Gypsy," but Juanita, along with the other two, was tried, found guilty, and sentenced to death—on the testimony of the third who was actually the "triggerman" (and who was later found insane and sent to a mental hospital, where he died).

She received three reprieves while awaiting death. Each time she was brought from the California Institution for Women to a death cell at San Quentin. The last time, when meeting with reporters, she pronounced a gypsy curse on them stating, "Six months from tomorrow, my blood will burn holes in [your] bodies."[5]

As she was preparing to enter the gas chamber, following what turned out to be a short-lived stay, Warden Duffy suddenly noticed the witnesses had not been returned. Turning to the Duchess he asked her if she wanted to return to her cell while all were reassembled. She said she would wait where she was. While there they discussed the weather for a few minutes and then proceeded to the gas chamber. Warden Duffy later wrote, "She was the only person I ever knew who could stand and talk about the weather while waiting to die."[6]

She requested to not be blindfolded and those at the execution noted that she stared at a bare light globe in the chamber as if she were hypnotized. She sat in one of the two green chairs in the octagonal gas-chamber known as the "diving bell." As the witnesses looked into the glass walled chamber they could faintly hear the metallic clank as the poisoned cyanide pellets ("eggs of death") dropped into the acid. According to those who had been at other executions in this same gas chamber, it took Juanita longer than others to die—11 minutes. It was later proposed this was due to the fumes being trapped in the folds of her green prison smock before reaching her nostrils.

When the stethoscope was placed on her chest, the pictures strapped to her bosom became visible. She had asked permission to have the pictures of her children and grandson taped underneath her dress. Actually, they were not her own children, but she had raised them as her own. In a final letter to the governor, asking for mercy, she explained that her 19-year-old daughter, "The Gypsy," had been found in a trash can. Seventeen-year-old Joseph was really her grandson (from a daughter she had given up for adoption), and 10-year-old Vincent was her niece's baby. She was raising all of them. While Juanita was awaiting death, her daughter had been in a Salvation Army home where she gave birth to a baby boy. It was his picture that was taped to the still chest of Juanita Spinelli—the first woman legally executed in California and the first by gas anywhere in the United States. She died on November 21, 1941.

North Carolina, as already noted, conducted the next two executions of women by gas. California's next one did not occur until the death of Louise Peete in 1947. She was one of the few women who had a previous homicide conviction—as well as an additional acquittal for homicide.

Louise Peete—"There Will Be No Screaming or Hysterics. I Am Not Built That Way."

Loveable Louise, the "Dowager of Tehachapi Prison," began her life as Lofie Louise Preslar, in 1883, in Bienville, Louisiana. But, she ended it as Louise Peete at the age of 64 in San Quentin's gas chamber. Four husbands she had married, four husbands had committed suicide, and one (perhaps as many as four) victims lie in her wake. She served 18 years for murdering a wealthy mining executive. Paroled in 1939 she lived with her female parole agent. When this agent died, of natural causes, Mrs. Peete (now having taken the interim name Anna B. Lee, after her favorite actress) was invited to move in with an elderly couple who had visited her while she was in prison. The wife was a retired social worker. Later the woman was found dead with a bullet hole in the back of her head, buried beneath the avocado tree in the garden. Her husband, with Mrs. Peete's "assistance," had been committed to a mental hospital, where he later died. Louise was tried for the wife's murder and sentenced to die.

During her previous prison sentence she was known to be a rather cultured person. In one interview she told a reporter, "There should be some way . . . of segregating the better educated, more refined women from those who have been brought up in close touch with life's slime and filth. They should be protected against being sullied by it."[7] It was always reported that she presented herself in "the grand manner" and that she was constantly putting on airs.

Warden Duffy described her before her death as looking like "a benign school teacher or president of the Tuesday Ladies' Sewing Circle."[8]

Commenting on her approaching execution, Louise Peete told reporters, "There will be no screaming or hysterics. I am not built that way."[9] Governor Earl Warren refused to grant a commutation of sentence. Louise entered the gas chamber on April 11, 1947, wearing a gray-and-burgundy print dress. She smiled and mouthed the words "thank you" to Warden Duffy.

In typifying Louise's life, author Miriam Aller DeFord quoted William Bolitho, who said she was one of those whose "self-compassion 'sucks the meaning out of every existence but their own,' whose lives are 'a serial adventure in which each episode is complete in itself, whose master-plot is known only to themselves.'"[10]

Perhaps it was a reporter who said it best. When a witness to her execution said, "At least she was gracious, even at the end," the reporter responded, "Yeah, that lady had manners that killed."[11]

Barbara Graham—"I Am Paying For a Life of Little Sins."

The picture on my wall that causes me the most reflection is that of Barbara Graham kissing her 2-year-old son Tommy goodbye just a few days before her execution. When asked if she had committed the crime—the killing of 63-year-old Mabel Monahan—she said, "I swear on Tommy's head I am innocent." She had two other sons, ages 12 and 14, by previous marriages, but it was Tommy she loved and would miss the most.

Barbara Elaine Wood Kielhammer Pueachel Newman Graham, "Bloody Babs," "Moll in Murder," notorious "Bad Girl," the "Icy Blonde," was sentenced to die along with two men, Emmett Perkins and Jack Santo. Both men had been convicted and sentenced to die for four previous murders and had been given a life sentence for one other. All-in-all they had been suspected in seven murders including those of three children. Barbara Graham was implicated as the killer in the Monahan murder by a man who agreed to testify against her in exchange for immunity. Barbara admitted she was a "bad girl" but denied any involvement in the "caper." She claimed, "I am paying for a life of little sins." Many of those who had known her agreed. She was known as a gambling shill, user of narcotics and prostitute. While a juvenile she was known as incorrigible, and a runaway, and sexually promiscuous as early as the age of 15. And why not? Many reasoned that both she and her mother were graduates of the Ventura School for Girls and had been through various institutions, reformatories, and jails. She craved the appearance of success, enjoyed nice things, and especially enjoyed music by Mozart and Stravinsky. All agreed she was not violent.

Mrs. Mabel Monahan, ex-mother-in-law of Luther Sherer, a Las Vegas casino owner, was thought to have large amounts of money and jewelry stored in her home in Burbank, California. Santo and Perkins, along with a man named True and another man named Shorter, accompanied by Barbara Graham, entered the Monahan home and demanded the valuables (which didn't exist). When Mrs. Monahan wouldn't (couldn't) turn them over, according to True's testimony, Barbara began to beat the old widow with the butt of a pistol. For his testimony, True was never charged with any crime. He died, later, in a shipwreck. Shorter, after talking briefly with the police, was kidnaped and never seen again. That left only Barbara Graham, Jack Santo and Emmett Perkins. All three were tried and sentenced to die.

It has been suggested by some investigators and writers that Barbara Graham was totally innocent, but framed by Santo and Perkins. Others still believe in her guilt. Among those facts on her side was trial evidence showing Mrs. Monahan had been beaten to death by a right-handed person—and Barbara was left-handed. Innocent or not, she didn't help herself when she attempted to bribe her cellmate to provide an alibi in her defense. As it turned out, the cellmate, "Shirley Olsen," was a policewoman planted in the cell to get evidence to use in court. Eventually, Barbara offered to pay $25,000 to another police plant if he would swear they were together on the night of the murder. She lost all credibility when this offer was divulged in court. Barbara's response, "Oh, have you ever been desperate? Do you know what it means not to know what to do?"[12] The jury showed no mercy. Some have postulated that Santo and Perkins implicated Graham because they believed a jury would never sentence her to death and if they didn't give her the death penalty, they couldn't give it to them, either. Others believe that she was totally innocent and was not even at the scene of the crime.

On the day before her execution, she arrived at San Quentin after a long drive from the California Institution for Women in Corona. She was "sick, tired and had a toothache." She wore red pajamas in her cell next to the gas chamber. During the night she had a milkshake and toward morning a hot fudge sundae. As the June 3, 1955, 10:00 a.m. time for her execution approached she dressed in a beige wool suit with covered buttons and wore brown pumps. Hanging from her ears were "bright sparkling baubles" and on her finger was her engagement band and wedding ring. Her execution was stayed until 10:27 a.m. and a new execution time of 10:45 a.m. was set. At 30 seconds after 10:43 a.m., as she was standing at her cell door and the blindfold was being put on, another stay was announced until ll:12 a.m. A new time of ll:30 a.m. was set. "Why do they torture me? I was ready to go at 10:00," she cried.[13] That was to be her final stay. She had asked for a blindfold so she wouldn't have to look at the people. Her death was quiet and without struggle. "In a situation like this, you don't moan, you don't beg, you don't plead—you try to be a woman."[14] She was buried by her husband, who told reporters, "I guess I'll have to tell Tommy that mummy moved some place too far away for us to visit her any more."[15]

Most experts concede that Barbara Graham didn't need to die. If she had pled guilty; if she had testified against the others involved; if she had shown more remorse—any of these could have saved her life. At one time she stated:

> The only way I can get any help. . .is if I say I did it—killed that old woman—and get my sentence commuted. But I'm not going to do it. I won't cop out. I won't come clean on something I didn't do.[16]

It was several years after Barbara Graham's execution that a movie starring Susan Hayward was made of her life and story. The title was "I Want To Live." It won Miss Hayward an Oscar. The title was perhaps not quite accurate. In one of Barbara's final interviews she told a reporter, "if I have to spend the rest of my life in prison—if I have to serve more than seven years—I want it the way it is. I'll take the gas chamber. Maybe that will be better for my kids."[17] It was her loyalty that cost her her life. "It's a gift I give people I think deserve it," she said in an interview with the *San Francisco Chronicle*. "You've got to help your friends."[18]

I'll remember Barbara because of the picture with Tommy, and because of her admonition, "Good people are always so sure they're right."

Elizabeth Duncan—"I Am Innocent. Where's Frank?"

"Ma" Duncan was the last woman executed in California. She died in the gas chamber August 8, 1962. At the time of her execution, the *Los Angeles Herald Examiner* made the following comparison:

> Three other women have been executed in California in the past 112 years. All were mothers, all were careful dressers, all were fiercely protective of their children, all had committed previous crimes.[19]

I met Frank Duncan. There is still bitterness over the events that led up to the execution of his mother. He was, in fact, pleading for her life at the time of her execution. Her last words were, "I am innocent. Where is Frank?" She was 58 at the time of her death. There were nine documented previous marriages and five children. Frank was the closest to her. Perhaps it was because of this that she hired two men to kill his pregnant bride, Olga, to whom he had been married for 5 months. The story, however, goes back much farther.

Elizabeth Gold Cogbill Gillis Sasso Satriano Solene Nigh Duncan (her real name, given to her at birth in Kansas City, was Hazel Sinclara Nigh) was a woman with a checkered past which included having worked as a madam in San Francisco. Her son Frank, an attorney, stayed by her and she was totally devoted to him. On the day before his 29th birthday the two of them had a spat and Ma overdosed on sleeping pills. Frank took her to the Santa Barbara Cottage Hospital where she was attended by nurse Olga Kupczyk, who had recently arrived from Canada. One thing led to another, Frank and Olga began dating, she became pregnant and, without telling Ma they were married. Elizabeth was furious and did everything she could to break up the marriage—even hiring an ex-con and going with him to court to impersonate Frank and Olga, to obtain an annulment. Next, Ma approached several people with various plans to kill Olga. Eventually she persuaded two dishwashers from a local cafe, former clients of Frank's—Luis Moya and Augustine Baldonado—to do the deed. Using the code name "Dorothy," she pawned her wedding ring and gave them $175 as a down payment.

On November 17, 1958, Olga disappeared from her home and on December 22, her body was found in a shallow grave. She had been strangled and pistol whipped, but died from suffocation after being buried alive. Moya and Baldonado quickly confessed; Ma was already in jail because of the investigation about the fraudulent annulment.

The trial was quite a media event. Spectators arrived early to get seats. The jury, when finally empanelled, consisted of eight women and four men with two alternates. The press duly noted what Mrs. Duncan wore, what expressions she had on her face, and what Frank had to say at the end of each day's testimony. When I spoke with Frank in his Los Angeles law office, we talked about the trial and eventual experience of his mother's execution. There is still bitterness, and no wonder. One newspaper reported:

> During the hearing, he heard himself called "liar," and "spineless jellyfish." He was accused of not loving his wife, going home to "mother" on his wedding night and leaving his wife when she was expecting a child because he could no longer have sexual relations. "I have nothing of which to be ashamed," he said. "A tragedy can happen to anyone. It doesn't mean life has to stop. I don't plan to join the foreign legion."[20]

Frank and I met in his law office in an old renovated building. The furnishings were classic and antique. In referring to the case, he remembered, "My God, the lies—unbelievable—total fabrications. If I could relive my life, I wouldn't do it."

The carnival atmosphere of the trial continued up to the last day. Spectators arrived as early as 5:00 a.m., some even paying $5 for places in line. One day of the trial, on the birthday of one of the deputy sheriffs who guarded the door, those waiting in line all greeted him by singing "Happy Birthday."

Each of the three defendants was tried separately. All three—Moya, and Baldonado, and Ma Duncan—were found guilty and sentenced to die. The triple execution took place in San Quentin's gas chamber on August 8, 1962. Mrs. Duncan was executed first. As she entered the gas chamber, the largest crowd of protestors since California's famous Caryl Chessman execution, 2 years previously, was gathering outside the prison walls. A few days earlier, as she left the California Institution for Women in Corona, she asked that her room be kept for her return. She waved goodbye and said, "See you tomorrow." Her appeals failed, however, and she died in the pale green gas chamber. Her last meal was steak and salad. She entered the chamber with dignity and composure. She wore a ". . . summery prison dress of red and white striped seersucker." Her dentures had been removed.

Governor Edmund Brown, an opponent of capital punishment, had refused to grant her clemency. (Some argued it was because of his bid for reelection against former Vice President Richard Nixon who was critical of his record in upholding California death sentences.) Frank, who was pleading for his mother's life at the time of her execution, claimed her body for burial. He still believed she was "the best mother a son could ever have."

The procedures for execution have, of necessity, been refined and formalized since these earlier times. The process is much more ritualized, wardens spend much less time with the condemned, visits are closely regulated and controlled, and the news media is kept at a greater distance. The public is usually told much less about the personal life of those being executed. Yet the decisions to execute remain as uncertain and capricious as ever.

The execution of Elizabeth (Ma) Duncan is very similar to the New York case of Dr. Alice Wynekoop—except Dr. Wynekoop was not executed. The similarities are, however, eerie.

COMPARISON CASE: DR. ALICE WYNEKOOP

In 1933, police were summoned to the home of the well respected Chicago physician Dr. Alice Wynekoop. In the basement, lying on an examination table, they found the nude body of Rheta Gardner Wynekoop, daughter-in-law of Dr. Wynekoop. Examining the body they found a bullet wound in her head. Dr. Wynekoop claimed a burglar had entered the home and killed her daughter-in-law. The police suspected otherwise. Eventually Alice offered another explanation in which she claimed to have been examining Rheta because of a pain in her side. She gave her some chloroform to help ease the pain during the examination. The girl quit breathing and, unable to resuscitate her, Dr. Wynekoop then shot her (while she was already dead) and concocted the burglary story to cover the "accidental death." This explanation was later withdrawn and she went to trial sticking with the burglary story.

Rheta had married Earle Wynekoop, the third of Dr. Wynekoop's children. Alice's husband, also a doctor, had died and left her to raise the three children. Earle was the youngest and the most spoiled. At the time of Earle's wife's death he was on a train headed for the Grand Canyon on a photography expedition—accompanied by an unattached young female companion. Earle was described as "a shiftless playboy and the darling of his hardworking mother."[21] Other accounts hinted at an unnatural, perverted, obsessive love between him and his mother. The prosecution suggested his mother would do anything to assist him—even killing a wife whom he no longer loved or wanted.

The trial must have seemed like a circus. The media reported 2,000 people—90% of them women—"stormed" the courthouse to see the trial. There was even a dowagers' special seating section where those women with connections were able to get reserve seating. Not since the Leopold and Loeb trial had anything this spectacular hit Chicago. The judge, Joseph David, was feisty, pacing the bench, interrupting the attorneys, and even correcting the grammar of the witnesses. Alice had innumerable "heart attacks." She was constantly attended by her daughter (also a physician) and a nurse—all seated at the defense table. She arrived at court, carried on a chair or in a wheelchair. Often the proceedings had to be interrupted for her to be revived or attended to. The dowagers paid close attention to her condition, either expressing concern as she slipped down in her chair or displeasure as she responded to her accusers. Whether sincere, or not, she played her part with dramatic flair. On one occasion, it was reported:

> [S]he seemed to breathe with difficulty and her face had a deathlike pallor beneath her veil. Dr. Wynekoop, of course, had stubbornly insisted the trial go on. As relatives and friends gathered around her she waved their protests aside. "For heaven's sake," she gasped, "I know I'm going to die and so do you all. But, look here now, my name must be cleared. Let's get on with this trial."[22]

The first trial was declared a mistrial. Her second trial ended in a sentence of guilty of first degree murder. The all-male jury had difficulty arriving at the sentence. One source suggested the 12 men on the jury became hungry and after 14 hours of deliberation, compromised on a 25 year sentence. She served 14 years, was paroled in 1949, and died 2 years later.

It is often hard to tell who should be executed and who should not. Perhaps if Ma Duncan had played things a little differently she might not have died.

Earle Wynekoop was kept away from the trial; Frank Duncan stayed by his mother, consoled her, and even carried her appeal before the governor of California. Earle disappeared. Frank has his own law practice in Southern California.

NOTES

1. *New York Times*, April 13, 1925.

2. *Salt Lake Tribune*, July 11, 1936.

3. Duffy, Clinton T., with Al Hirshberg. 1962. *88 Men And Two Women*. Garden City, N.Y.: Doubleday & Company, Inc., p. 135.

4. *Detroit News*, November 21, 1941, p.1.

5. Ibid.

6. Duffy, op.cit., p.141.

7. deFord, Miriam Allen. 1965. *Murderers Sane & Mad*. New York: Avon Books, p.98–99.

8. Duffy, op.cit., p.132.

9. Nash, Robert Jay. 1980. Murder, America. New York: Simon and Schuster, p.262.

10. deFord, op.cit., p.101.

11. Nash, op.cit., p.263.

12. deFord, op.cit., p.87.

13. *Herald Examiner*, June 4, 1955.

14. Nash, Robert Jay. 1973. *Bloodletters And BadMen*. New York: M. Evans and Company, Inc., p.225.

15. deFord, op.cit., p.89.

16. *San Francisco Chronicle*, October 18, 1953.

17. Ibid., October 18, 1953.

18. *San Francisco Chronicle*, October 15, 1953.

19. *Los Angeles Herald Examiner*, August 8, 1962.

20. Ibid.

21. Nash, 1973, op.cit.,p.392.

22. *New York Times*, January 20, 1934, p.32.

Part Four

Federal Executions of Women

On my now crowded wall is a picture of four people hanging from a gallows next to a high brick wall. There are several soldiers standing along the wall and many spectators gathered in the small yard around the gallows. Some are in uniform; others in civilian dress. The picture shows several people carrying umbrellas. The date is July 7, 1865. Each of the four hanging on the gallows has a white canvas hood over the head and each has been bound with what seems to be white strips of cloth around the arms and legs. It is a unique picture; unique also is the fact that the body hanging on the far left is a woman.

Mary Surratt—"If I Had Two Lives to Give, I'd Give One Gladly to Save Mrs. Surratt."

Mary Surratt was the first woman executed by the federal government. There have been three in all—Mary Surratt, executed on July 7, 1865, for her involvement in the Lincoln assassination; Ethel Rosenberg, executed with her husband, Julius, on June 19, 1953, for giving atomic bomb secrets to the Russians; and Bonnie Brown Heady, executed with her lover, Carl Hall, on December 18, 1953, for violation of the Lindberg Law (kidnapping and killing of 6-year-old Bobby Greenlease).

Mary was the owner and operator of a boarding house in Washington, D.C. Recently I enjoyed a Chinese meal at a restaurant in Washington, D.C.'s Chinatown. As I entered there was a brass plaque on the wall identifying the site as the location of Mary Surratt's boarding house—604 H Street NW.

Her 20-year-old son became acquainted with John Wilkes Booth and agreed to be a part of the plot being hatched by Booth to assassinate Lincoln. As far as is known, Mrs. Surratt was not involved in the actual assassination.

It was claimed the plot was organized in her boarding house and, the only other connection, a conspirator named Lewis Powell (a.k.a. Payne) who had attempted to kill Secretary of State Seward, ran to her boarding house to hide and was later arrested there, along with Mrs. Surratt. She was sentenced to die although the case was never made against her. On the gallows, Paine appealed, "If I had two lives to give, I'd give one gladly to save Mrs. Surratt. I know that she is innocent, and would never die in this way if I hadn't been found in her house. She knew nothing about the conspiracy at all. . . ."[1] Her son John was never punished for his involvement.

The execution took place in the Old Penitentiary in Washington, D.C. The gallows, erected the night before, was described as:

> . . . twenty feet long, fifteen feet wide and ten feet high to the floor and twenty to the beam. A beam ran through the center of the platform, east and west, and upon each side of this beam and on the west side of the platform was a drop. Each drop was six feet long by four feet wide and over each drop and suspended from the top beam hung two ropes made of strong hemp, the slip noose of each rope being formed of nine twists and a knot . . . A few feet southeast of the scaffold four graves, each one four feet deep, seven feet long and three feet wide had been dug and were intended for the reception of the remains of the condemned prisoners. Beside these graves the coffins, made of plain pine boards, had been placed.[2]

Before her execution Mary Surratt was visited by her daughter Annie who prayed with her most of the morning. Just before leaving, Mrs. Surratt instructed her daughter as to the disposition of her possessions after her execution. Wearing a "black alpaca dress and . . . a veil over her face," Mary Surratt was brought out first. She walked steadily until reaching the first step leading up to the gallows. As the noose was placed over her head there was some concern that she might faint. To those assisting her she said, "Please don't let me fall."[3] After the supports were kicked away, all four of the condemned dangled from their ropes. August Mencken, who wrote about hangings, said that "A shudder passed through the frame of Mrs. Surratt, but there was no other motion except a nervous twitching of the hands. . . ." The bodies were being taken down, and at that time "as the rope was cut, [Mrs. Surratt's] head . . . fell forward upon her breast and an individual standing by made the heartless remark, 'She makes a good bow.' He was properly rebuked by an officer standing by."[4] According to the surgeon who examined the bodies, none of the necks had been broken. All had apparently strangled to death as each hung suspended from the rope.

Mrs. Surratt was the first woman to be executed by the federal government; there were to be two more who would follow—but it would be many years until Ethel Rosenberg followed.

Ethel Rosenberg—"Always Remember That We Were Innocent and Could Not Wrong Our Conscience."

On Sunday, November 2, 1986, the Associated Press reported:

> Abel Meeropol, a lyricist who adopted the sons of convicted spies Julius and Ethel Rosenberg, died Wednesday at his home. He was 83 years of age. In 1957, the lyricist adopted Michael and Robert Rosenberg whose parents were convicted in 1951 of passing atomic bomb secrets to the Soviet Union. The parents were executed in 1953.

The sons, who were placed with and eventually adopted by Mr. Meeropol and his wife after the execution, have continued trying to prove their parents' innocence.

Robert and Michael Rosenberg Meeropol dedicated their 1975 book, *We Are Your Sons: The Legacy of Ethel and Julius Rosenberg* to Abel Meeropol and Anne Meeropol:

> To the memory of Anne Meeropol, who was a creative, courageous person and a strong, dynamic and loving parent.
> To Abel Meeropol, who continues to struggle with energy and foresight; his gentleness and humor gave and still give us laughter.

Robert and Michael Rosenberg were ages 6 and 10 respectively, when their parents died in New York's electric chair. It was a trial and execution born out of the postwar concern with Russia and the heightened "cold war" furor. The judge in the case refused to give any support to pleas of mercy and clemency. To him, their crime was very serious, "I still feel that their crime was worse than murder."[5] President Dwight D. Eisenhower felt the same way. In refusing to grant any clemency, he stated:

> The nature of the crime for which they have been found guilty and sentenced far exceeds that of the taking of the life of another citizen; it involves the deliberate betrayal of the entire nation and could very well result in the death of many, many thousands of innocent citizens. By their act these two individuals have in fact betrayed the cause of freedom for which free men are fighting and dying at this very hour.[6]

Julius and Ethel Rosenberg came to the death house in Ossining, New York, through a circuitous route that included Klaus Fuchs, arrested as a Soviet agent in England; Harry Gold, a biochemist; Allan Nunn, part of a Canadian espionage ring; Anatoli Yacovley, Soviet vice consul in New York; Morton Sobell and Mrs. Rosenberg's brother, David Greenglass, who had worked at the New Mexico installation where the first atomic bomb was developed.

Their trial took place in the environment of the Korean War, with Senator Joseph McCarthy at the peak of his anti-Communism "Red Scare" campaign and at a time when conflict with Russia was believed to be inevitable. There are those who question the evidence against the Rosenbergs and arguments can be made in both directions. The key issue, however, was whether they should have been executed.

Harry Truman was President when the Rosenbergs appealed for clemency but he left office 10 days later and it was up to the newly elected President Eisenhower to decide. Many countries and famous people joined the appeals, including Albert Einstein. All were in vain. The Rosenberg execution was scheduled for June 19, 1953.

On that day, the Rosenbergs were allowed to visit with each other through a mesh screen. One of their final acts was to write a letter to their two sons:

Dearest Sweethearts, my most precious children,
Only this morning it looked like we might be together again after all. Now that this cannot be, I want so much for you to know all that I have come to know. Unfortunately, I may write only a few simple words; the rest your own lives must teach you, even as mine taught me.

At first, of course, you will grieve bitterly for us, but you will not grieve alone. That is our consolation and it must eventually be yours.

Eventually, too, you must come to believe that life is worth the living. Be comforted that even now, with the end of ours slowly approaching, that we know this with a conviction that defeats the executioner!

Your lives must teach you, too, that good cannot really flourish in the midst of evil; that freedom and all the things that go to make up a truly satisfying and worthwhile life, must sometimes be purchased very dearly. Be comforted then that we were serene and understood with the deepest kind of understanding, that civilization had not as yet progressed to the point where life did not have to be lost for the sake of life; and that we were comforted in the sure knowledge that others would carry on after us.

We wish we might have had the tremendous joy and gratification of living our lives out with you. Your Daddy who is with me in the last momentous hours, sends his heart and all the love that is in it for his dearest boys. Always remember that we were innocent and could not wrong our conscience.

We press you close and kiss you with all our strength.
Lovingly,
Daddy and Mommy
Julie Ethel[7]

An open telephone line was kept with an FBI agent standing by throughout the execution should either of the two confess and tell about the other conspirators. They were promised their death sentence would be commuted should they be willing to tell all.

Julius was executed first and was followed a few minutes later by Ethel. There had been no last meal. The time of execution had been moved up to 8:00 p.m. to be done before the beginning of the Jewish Sabbath. Ethel entered quietly, wearing a dark green dress with white polka dots. She looked straight ahead as the leather mask was placed over her face. By law, only five witnesses were allowed at a federal execution; three of these were news reporters. This was the first federal execution of a woman since the hanging of Mary Surratt.

As Ethel was taken from her cell the rabbi said, "Ethel, for the sake of the children who need you, will you say something which can still save you? Must this tragedy be completed?" She responded, "I have nothing to say. I am ready."[8]

Once the current began to course through her body, she stiffened, and was lifted off the oak seat. Her hands opened and closed and then she slowly sank down into the chair. Three times the current was applied. On examination by the attending physician it was found she was still alive. After consultations between the warden and the executioner, current was applied two more times and she was pronounced dead. For Julius it took 2 minutes and 45 seconds. Ethel died after 4 minutes and 30 seconds—she had actually been pronounced dead after the Sabbath had begun.[9]

Joseph Francel, who 14 years earlier had been named as New York's state executioner, received $300 for the job—$150 per execution.

Bonnie Brown Heady—"I'd Rather Die Than Be Poor."

The third and, to date, last federal execution of a woman was that of 41-year-old Bonnie Brown Heady. She died along with Carl Austin Hall in Missouri's gas chamber on December 18, 1953. They died 29 days after being sentenced and 81 days after their crime under the 1923 Lindberg Law. Mrs. Heady, posing as an aunt, went to the private Catholic school of 6-year-old Bobby Greenlease and told the nuns that her sister, Bobby's mother, was in the hospital with a heart attack. The mother wanted to see her son and Mrs. Heady was there to pick him up. He went with her quietly and was killed within hours, buried in a shallow grave at the home of Mrs. Heady. A ransom note for $600,000 was later delivered to his parents.

A nationwide manhunt ensued. The FBI, under the Lindberg Law, was prohibited from entering the case until after 7 days. (After this case, the law was changed to allow immediate entry of the FBI in kidnaping cases.) Nothing turned up until a suspicious taxi driver alerted the authorities to the location of a Carl Austin Hall who was passing around a lot of money. He was arrested in his hotel room with close to $300,000. He led authorities to Bonnie Brown

Heady, where he had abandoned her, drunk in a motel room with $2,000. Both were tried and sentenced to die in Missouri's gas chamber. The remaining $300,000 was never recovered.

Bonnie was the ex-wife of a livestock merchant from St. Joseph; their marriage lasted 20 years. Hall was the only living son of an influential attorney from Pleasanton, Kansas. Both entered the gas chamber after spending their last hours together enjoying a meal of fried chicken, mashed potatoes and gravy, salad with Roquefort cheese dressing, and rolls. She wore a green cotton dress with slippers. After being seated in the chair, her last audible words were, "Is my dress pulled down?" They died side-by-side with the warden as executioner. According to one news report, their greed over $600,000 had cost them their lives and it had cost the government exactly $4.40 in chemicals to do it. Their last breath had been taken while carolers, outside the death house, were serenading the inmates in a pre-Christmas celebration.

COMPARISON CASES: JUDITH COPLON, THE "PETTICOAT SPY" AND MILDRED GILLARS, "AXIS SALLY"

On March 4, 1949, Judith Coplon, along with Soviet United Nations Engineer Valentin A. Gubitchev, was arrested on charges of espionage. When arrested, Coplon was carrying in her purse information about 34 ongoing FBI cases, including some files that had been planted by the FBI to catch her.

The daughter of a Jewish toy merchant, Coplon was a graduate of Barnard College where she majored in history. After working her way up the ladder of the Justice Department—from the War Division to the Criminal Division— she eventually became the department's expert on Communism. When it seemed confidential information was being leaked, the trail led to her. Investigation showed she took regular monthly trips to New York where she met with Gubitchev.

Quickly dubbed the "Petticoat Spy" she was tried first in Washington D.C.—which she referred to as a "loyalty-oath-ridden town."[10] The charge was espionage conspiracy. She was found guilty and before sentencing stated:

> I understand I could plead for mercy. That I will not do. To me pleading for mercy would be an admission of guilt.[11]

She was sentenced to the Federal Prison for a term of 40 months to 10 years. Later, tried in New York on espionage conspiracy charges, she was again found guilty and sentenced to 20 years in prison. At her New York sentencing the judge lectured her. . . . :

You have brought dishonor upon the name you bear. You have been disloyal to the country which nourished you, helped you acquire an education, and placed you in high trust and confidence. You have proved yourself an ungrateful daughter.[12]

Gubitchev fared rather well throughout the trial process. He was given 15 years in jail—suspended on condition he leave the United States and never return.

Interestingly, Judith Coplon never did go to prison. The U.S. Supreme Court turned down a motion for retrial and, in 1950 (2 years before the Rosenbergs' execution) her New York conviction was overturned by the Appeals Court.

It is also of interest to note that, at this same time, several trials of other spies were going on, including that of two women known as "Tokyo Rose"— none of which resulted in death sentences.

January 25, 1949, marked the opening day of trial for Mildred E. Gillars, known as "Axis Sally." She was 48 years old, a native of Portland, Maine, and educated at Hunter College. Actually, it was her experience at Hunter College that brought her under the tutelage of one of her professors, Max O. Koishewitz. She fell in love with him. Her defense argued it was less love and more his "hypnotic spell that influenced her and led her to follow him to Germany where he used her to broadcast 'sugar-coated pills of propaganda.'" This propaganda included visits to hospitals and concentration camps where she presented herself as a nurse for the Red Cross, interested in sending messages from American soldiers home to their families. These "messages" were later altered to serve the propaganda interests of Nazi Germany. She was also involved in a radio production in which she took the part of an American mother from Ohio who spoke with her son through a dream and found out he had been killed while crossing the English Channel. Broadcasting over station ZDZ Berlin, she conducted chats with the girls at home explaining the "reason for my being here in Berlin [and] not sitting at home with you at the little sewing bees knitting socks for our men over in French North Africa," is because:

I'm not on the side of President Roosevelt . . . and his Jewish friends and his British friends because I've been brought up to be a 100 percent American girl.[13]

She also gave the message to soldiers that their "sweethearts were running around with the 4-F's back home."[14] (4F was the Selective Service classification given to those males exempt from or unable to serve in the military during World War II.)

At trial the prosecution charged she got a "sadistic joy" out of making her broadcasts. The defense relied on the claim she was under the influence of

Professor Koischewitz and on her fear for her life if she didn't cooperate with the Nazis. The jury deliberated 17 hours and 20 minutes and eventually found her guilty of treason—which carried the possibility of the death penalty. A *New York Times* editorial stated:

> [W]e have never executed any civilian for treason in this country in time of peace, except for John Brown, and we usually go easier with women than with men.[15]

Axis Sally was sentenced to serve 10 to 30 years in prison and fined $10,000. Three years later Ethel Rosenberg died in New York's electric chair.

NOTES

1. Nash, 1973, op.cit., p.76.
2. Mencken, August. 1942. *By The Neck: A Book of Hangings*. New York: Hastings House, p.136.
3. Ibid., p.137.
4. Menchen's book, p.139.
5. *New York Times*, February 12, 1953.
6. Ibid.
7. Meeropol, Robert and Michael. 1975. *We Are Your Sons: The Legacy of Ethel and Julius Rosenberg*. New York: Ballentine Books, p.264–265.
8. Nizer, Louis. 1973. *The Implosion Conspiracy*. Greenwich, Conn.: Fawcett Publications, Inc., pp.529–530.
9. Ibid., p.532.
10. *New York Times*, July 2, 1949, p.1.
11. Ibid.
12. 1974. *Crimes And Punishment: A Pictoral Encyclopedia of Aberrant Behavior*. Paulgon, England: BPC Publishing Limited, p.140.
13. *New York Times*, January 28, 1949, p.18.
14. *New York Times*, March 10, 1949, p.1.
15. *New York Times*, March 11, 1949, p.24.

Part Five

The Last Two of the 20th Century

In 1997, three executions were scheduled in the United States during the month of January. Actually, all three were scheduled for the same 24-hour period.

Delaware was scheduled to hang Billy Bailey, who killed an elderly couple. It was to be the state's first hanging in 50 years. This hanging hiatus engendered a certain amount of uncertainty as to the process and whether or not a competent hangman could be located.

Utah was scheduled to execute John Albert Taylor by firing squad. Taylor was sentenced to die for the rape/strangulation of a young girl who had been killed the day before her twelfth birthday.

And, the state of Illinois was prepared for the lethal injection execution of Guinevere Garcia–who wanted to die. It would be Illinois' first execution of a woman in 57 years.

Delaware did hang Billy Bailey and Utah did shoot John Albert Taylor. Illinois, however, did not execute Guin Garcia. Instead, Governor Jim Edgar commuted her sentence. Why was Guin Garcia's sentence commuted–even when she wished to die–and why, less than a year later, did Governor George W. Bush of Texas and Governor Lawton Chiles of Florida refuse to grant clemency to Karla Faye Tucker and Judy Buenoano? Part Seven will examine in more detail how governors deal with the clemency and commutation decisions they are called upon to make.

Karla Faye Tucker–"Here She Comes Baby Doll, She's All Yours."

Texas had not executed a woman during the 20th century. Karla Faye Tucker became the first woman to be executed in Texas since Chipita Rodriguez died by hanging on Friday 13, 1863, for killing a horse trader. It is said Chipita's ghost, with frayed rope around her neck, still can be seen wandering the countryside whenever a Texas woman is sentenced to die.

Karla Faye Tucker was sentenced to die for the 1983 pickax killing of Jerry Dean and Deborah Thornton. (Actually, the weapon was a 15 pound mattock.) Her co-defendant, Daniel Garrett, was also sentenced to be executed, but he died in prison in 1993 of liver disease.

Karla Faye was referred to in some news reports as the ". . .nicest woman on death row." Others referred to her as the "pick axe killer." She referred to herself as "born again." While on death row she had found religion. In her own words:

It was in October, three months after I had been locked up, when a ministry came to the jail and I went to the services, that night accepting Jesus into my heart.[1]

While in prison, she married Dana Brown, a prison minister. They were never allowed any physical contact. He was present at her execution.

This religion factor in Karla Faye Tucker's case opened an interesting debate regarding the issue of "redemption" and "retribution." Should the fact that this one-time drug user, prostitute, delinquent, had changed her life and found redemption, provide grounds for clemency, or was the retributive aspect of the death penalty more important in seeing that the demands of justice be met?

Pope John Paul II, Pat Robertson (TV evangelist) and others argued for commutation because of her ". . .metamorphosis from a drug-crazed teenage prostitute to a soft-spoken young woman who would be content with a life sentence."[2]

On the retribution side was Governor George W. Bush and the Texas Board of Pardons and Paroles. The board voted 16-0 to deny clemency and the governor, by statute, could only grant a one-time 30-day reprieve in order to allow the board to reconsider its decision. During his three years in office, he had never done this in the cases of the 59 men he allowed to be executed.

Tucker's appeal for clemency was actually two-fold. First, she argued her sentence should be commuted because of her conversion and the changes in her life. Second, she argued the Texas clemency process was flawed.

When questioned about the "gender factor," a spokesperson for Governor Bush responded, "The gender of the murderer did not make any difference to the victim."[3] As far as the conversion factor, Victor Rodriguez, chair of the Board of Pardons and Paroles, stated:

When a jury assesses a death penalty on someone, they made a conclusion that says, "You can never prove to us that you will be different." That's the essence of a death penalty.[4]

Upon hearing this statement, David Batsford, one of Karla Faye Tucker's attorneys, responded, "Texas has no mercy."

On February 3, 1998, the Associated Press quoted Governor Bush:

> Like many touched by this case, I have sought guidance through prayer. I have concluded judgements about the heart and soul of an individual on death row are best left to a higher authority.[5]

He concluded by stating, "May God bless Karla Faye Tucker and may God bless her victims and their families."

While all of this was going on, in the Texas red brick prison unit ("The Walls"), the execution process was in full swing. Outside, protestors' signs read:

> "Forget injection. Use a pickax."
> "Axe and you shall receive."
> "Justice is blind to religion."

Inside, Karla Faye was finishing a last meal of sliced peaches, a banana and a green salad. She had been flown to Huntsville the previous day from the women's death row unit in Gatesville, where six other women awaited their own executions.

As time for execution drew closer, one of those waiting to be a witness was Richard Thornton, the husband of the victim, Deborah Thornton. Wearing a yellow dandelion given him by his granddaughter, he looked up as Karla Faye was strapped to the gurney and whispered, "Here she comes baby doll. She's all yours. The world's a better place."[6]

From the gurney, Tucker looked at those gathered to witness the execution. To the victim's families she said, "I would like to say to all of you, the Thornton family and Jerry Dean's family that I am so sorry. I hope God will give you peace with this." To her husband, Dana Brown, she said, "Baby, I love you." To Ron Carlson, Deborah Thornton's brother, she stated, "Ron, give Peggy a hug for me." To everyone in general, her last words were, "Everybody has been so good to me. I love all of you very much. . .I am going to be face to face with Jesus now. Warden Baggett, thank all of you so much. You have been so good to me. I love all of you very much. I will see you all when you get there. I will wait for you."[7]

Karla Faye Tucker died at the age of 38. Her crime was committed 15 years earlier, when she was 23 years old. Witnesses described her death by stating, "She coughed twice, let out a soft groan, then fell silent."[8] Another witness recorded:

> As the drugs began taking effect, she gasped slightly twice, then let out a five-to-ten second wheeze as the air escaped from her lungs. Her eyes remained

nearly wide open. Her mouth remained slightly open. She was pronounced dead at 6:45 p.m.[9]

Why all the attention to this execution? Obviously, the media helped muster national and international attention and sympathy because of her ". . . sex and her doe-eyed good looks."[10] A University of Houston law professor identified five characteristics that Karla Faye had which he felt contributed to making her a media sensation, ". . . she was a woman, white, attractive, articulate and a Christian." According to him, some other women on death row have four of these characteristics, others three, but few have all five.[11]

Judi Buenoano–"Via Con Dios"

Judi Buenoano had two of the five characteristics–female and white. She was a Christian but didn't trade on that, she was not particularly attractive nor articulate; and she drowned her teenage paraplegic son. It is pretty difficult to enlist much sympathy for a mother who kills her handicapped son.

The media was not particularly interested. Judi died just days after Karla Faye Tucker, but there was little attention paid to her execution. Labeled the "Black Widow," Judi Buenoano spent her last days writing letters and crocheting blankets and baby clothing. Buenoano is the Spanish equivalent of "Goodyear," her husband's name, which she took after his death.

Like Texas, Florida had not executed a woman for over 100 years. The last Florida female execution was a slave known as Celia. She was hanged in 1848 for helping two male slaves kill their owner, who was found stabbed to death.

Judi Buenoano's fiancé, John Gentry, was the victim of a car bombing in Pensacola, Florida in 1983. Because Judi had given him "vitamins" prior to the bombing incident, and they had made him sick, she became a suspect. Further investigation led to the discovery of her other two killings. James Goodyear, her first husband, died of arsenic poisoning in 1971, three months after he returned from a year's tour of duty in Vietnam. Michael Goodyear, her 19-year-old son who was partially paralyzed and wore heavy leg and arm braces, drowned in 1980, when the canoe he was riding in with his mother and sister capsized. He was wearing no life jacket and it was charged by the prosecution that his mother pushed him out of the canoe. It was even hinted that she caused his original paralysis by arsenic poisoning.

For these two deaths, she was tried, found guilty of murder and sentenced to die. Colorado prosecutors found evidence she had also poisoned her boyfriend, Bobby Joe Norris, in Trinidad, Colorado, but chose not to charge her.

There was little, if any, media attention. CNN's Greta Van Susteren conducted an on-camera TV interview from Florida's death row. Judi came across friendly, fairly open, but distant. The "sympatisch" factor was not there. She did not become the darling of the media. She did not endear herself to born-again Christians and, she did not look young and beautiful. She was a hard woman who had lived a hard life–and she killed her crippled teenage son for insurance money.

Even Governor Lawton Chiles, a Democrat, couldn't find grounds for mercy. A spokesperson for the governor said, "To the governor these cases [clemency appeals] aren't about gender, they are about justice."[12]

The 75-year-old electric chair sat ready. Out of 36 total condemned inmates awaiting execution in Florida, six of them were women.

After 13 years on death row, Judi went to her death on March 30, 1998–the 37th birthday of her son, had he lived. She made no last statement. Although she told the CNN interviewer her last words would be, "Via Con Dios," when asked if she had anything to say, she responded, "No, sir."

Wearing dark blue slacks and a white shirt with head shaved, she closed her eyes as she was strapped to the chair.[13] Maintaining her innocence to the end, witnesses reported she "squeezed her eyes and kept them shut. The power was turned on at 7:08 a.m.–smoke curled up from her right leg throughout the 38 second execution. She was pronounced dead at 7:13 a.m."[14]

Judi, like Karla, responded to a questionnaire I sent regarding conditions on death row for women. Judi continued to correspond with my research assistant, who even made a visit to her on Florida's death row. Prior to her execution, we corresponded again. Her last letter to me expressed gratitude for my letters and suggested I contact the prison for permission to attend her execution. She was probably not aware that Florida does not allow the inmate to choose her own witnesses.

In their book about Judi's crime, Anderson and McGehee included a poem that nicely summarizes her life:

Don't be fooled by me, Don't be fooled by the face I wear, for I wear a thousand masks, masks that I'm afraid to take off, and none of them are me. . . . My surface may seem smooth, but my surface is my mask. Beneath this lies no complacence. Beneath dwells the real me in confusion, in fear, in aloneness. But I hide this. I don't want anybody to know it. I panic at the thought of my weakness and fear of being exposed. That's why I frantically create a mask to hide behind. A nonchalant, sophisticated facade to help me pretend, to shield me from the glance that knows. But such a glance will not be followed by acceptance and love. I'm afraid you'll think less of me, that you'll laugh at me, and your laugh would kill me. I'm afraid that deep down I'm nothing, that I'm no good, and that you will see this and reject me. So, I play my game, my desperate game, and so begins the parade of masks, and my life becomes a front. . . . I idly chatter to you in the suave tones of surface talk. I tell you everything that is really nothing and nothing of what is everything, of what is crying within me. So when I go through my routine, do not be fooled by what I'm saying. Please listen carefully and try to hear what I'm not saying, what I'd like to be able to say, what for survival I need to say, but what I can't say. . . ."[15]

Perhaps this could be said of all the women in this book.

COMPARISON CASE: GUINEVERE GARCIA, "STAY OUT OF MY CASE. STAY OUT OF MY LIFE."

Karla Faye Tucker and Judi Buenoano both wanted clemency and didn't get it. Guinevere (Guin) Garcia didn't want clemency, but got it. Her death sentence was commuted to life in prison without possibility of parole by Governor Edgar, on January 16, 1996. She had already ordered her last meal–a deep dish pizza.

Guin Garcia's life had been one of chaos. At the age of 14 months, she watched her alcoholic mother plunge to her death from their apartment window. At age 15, she was gang raped by a group of teenage boys. At age 16, her grandfather gave written permission for her to marry an Iranian immigrant so he could get citizenship. He paid her $1,500. Before she turned 17, she went to work as a stripper. When she was 18, desperate and drunk, she smothered her 11-month-old daughter, Sara.[16] For this crime, she received a 20 year sentence.

Only four months after her release, she killed her estranged husband, George. He was her second husband, 30 years her senior, a former client from her prostitution days, but a man who offered her a place to live so she could be paroled. Some claim she was constantly physically and sexually abused. There were even stories that he had taken a blade and cut her genitalia. Whatever the situation, she killed him while trying to rob him and this time she was sentenced to die by lethal injection.

Guin Garcia wanted to die. She refused to appeal her sentence and told people, "Stay out of my case. Stay out of my life." Once she had made the decision to die, quit the appeals process and accepted her fate, she said:

I started eating and sleeping. I started forgiving people whom I had hated, and I started asking for forgiveness from those people who I had not asked for forgiveness from before.[17]

The *Chicago Tribune* stated, "Garcia said that death would be merciful compared with the prospect of sharing a prison cell with the demons of her life."[18]

But, it was not to be. Governor Jim Edgar thought otherwise. Although he had previously granted clemency to seven battered women convicted of murder, he had never granted clemency to someone on death row. In commuting her sentence, he said:

> . . . this is not the kind of case I had in mind when I voted as a legislator to restore the death penalty . . . it is also not the kind of case that typically results in a death sentence in Illinois.[19]

He acknowledged what he did was:

> . . . contrary to Guinevere Garcia's express wish to let the execution go forward–a wish she has repeated several times forcefully. But it is not the state's responsibility to carry out the wishes of a defendant. It is the state's responsibility to assure that the death penalty continues to be administered properly.[20]

A statement read by his attorney explained:

> It was not . . . because she was a woman or a battered and sexually abused woman. It was just that it was not right . . . as long as other people convicted of more heinous crimes have eluded the death penalty in Illinois.[21]

He later stated:

> I have wrestled with this decision and deliberated at length. Horrible as was her crime, it is an offense comparable to those that judges and jurors have determined over and over again should not be punishable by death.[22]

Finally, he stated:

> It is a decision that I made that I have to live with the rest of my life. I am convinced this is the right decision. I do think she should spend the rest of her life in prison and based on her comments, that might be a worse sentence to her.[23]

Even though he was generous to Guinevere, he still left four other women on Illinois' death row. And, what was Guin's response upon hearing the news? "Thank God this happened."

Some have been so bold as to suggest clemency, in this instance, may not have been so merciful. One person postulated:

It's very peculiar . . . she will have to grieve for the gift of life. She apparently viewed her execution as a gift, and not getting it is a loss for her, she will probably feel angry and some sadness and resignation. And, at some point, she will have to deal with the reality of the future, as we all do.[24]

NOTES

1. From a letter by Tucker, written to Governor Bush, asking for clemency. *USA Today*, February 3, 1998. P. 2A.

2. *Salt Lake Tribune*, February 4, 1998, p. 5.

3. *New York Times*, February 3, 1998, p. 1.

4. Interview on A&E's *Dead Woman Walking* video.

5. *New York Times*, February 3, 1998, p. 1.

6. *Salt Lake Tribune*, February 4, 1998, p. 1.

7. *Karla Faye Tucker*, Internet home page, http://www.straughtway.org/karla/karla.htm.

8. *Salt Lake Tribune*, February 4, 1998, p. 1.

9. Michael Graezyk, *USA Today*, February 4, 1998, p. 4A.

10. *New York Times*, February 4, 1998, p.1.

11. University of Houston Law Professor David R. Dow, *New York Times*, February 5, 1998, p. 12.

12. *New York Times*, February 10, 1998, p. 10.

13. *New York Times*, March 31, 1998, p. 16.

14. *Ogden Standard Examiner*, March 31, 1998, p. A1.

15. Apparently taken from Judi's journal, as partially quoted in *Bodies of Evidence*, Chris Anderson and Sharon McGehee (St. Martin's Paperbacks, 1991).

16. *New York Times*, January 8, 1996, p. 8.

17. Ibid., p. 8.

18. *Chicago Tribune*, January 17, 1996.

19. *New York Times*, January 16, 1996, p. 8.

20. Ibid.

21. *Chicago Tribune*, January 17, 1996.

22. *Chicago Tribune*, January 17, 1996.

23. Ibid.

24. Ibid.

Part Six

The New Century

While the 20th century came quietly to an end with only two executions of women in the last decade, the 21st century got off to a quick start only days into the new century. It only took 55 days into this new century for the state of Texas to execute Betty Lou Beets.

EXECUTIONS OF WOMEN: 20TH AND 21ST CENTURY

Not only did the pace of female executions increase with the beginning of the 21st century, but several issues from the past century brought closure.

"The Brother: The Untold Story of Atomic Spy David Greenglass and How He Sent His Sister, Ethel Rosenberg, to the Electric Chair"[1]

With the publication of his book, *The Brother*, Sam Roberts, through interviews with David Greenglass, discloses the fact that Greenglass falsely implicated his sister, Ethel Rosenberg, in order to protect his wife, Ruth.

> "I seldom use the word *sister* anymore; I've just wiped it out of my mind. . . .I told them the story and left her [Ethel] out of it, right? But my wife put her in it. So what am I gonna do, call my wife a liar? My wife is my wife. I mean, I don't sleep with my sister, you know."[2]

Ethel Rosenberg, along with her husband, was executed as an atomic spy on June 19, 1953.

"State Gives Full Pardon to Executed Maid in '45"[3]

In the first and only case of its kind, Lena Baker who was executed in 1945, received a posthumous pardon by the state of Georgia. Sentenced to die for killing her white employer, E. B. Knight, she claimed self-defense. But, as a

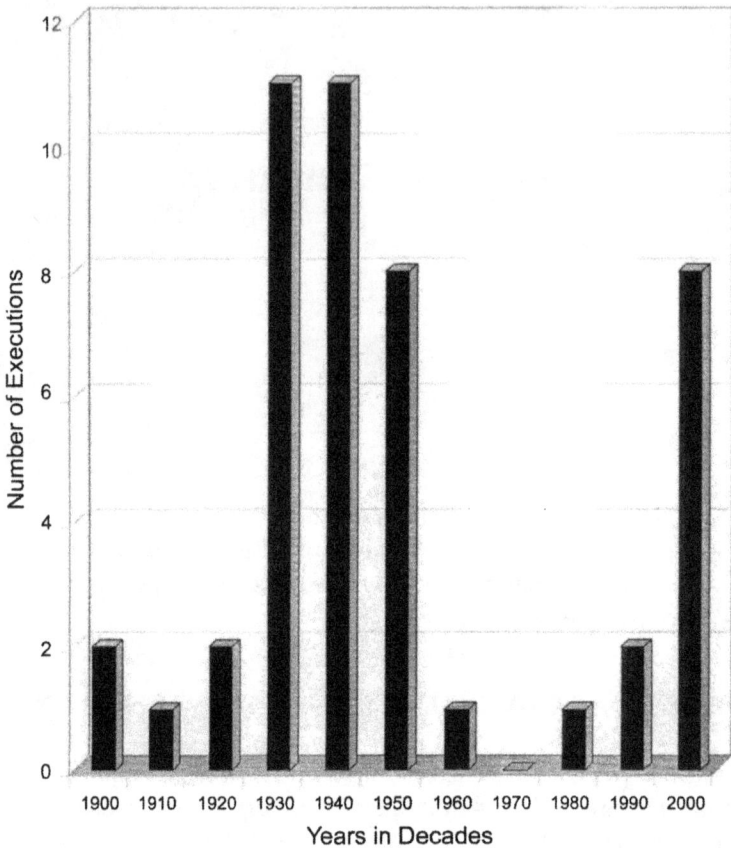

Figure 1. Executions by Decade

Black woman in the southern state of Georgia, the all white jury found her guilty. Lena Baker maintained her innocence to the end in her final statement saying, "What I done, I did in self-defense."[4]

Her 69 year old daughter, who was unable to travel to the ceremony, wrote:

"To each and everyone here today that made this day possible, I want to thank you from the bottom of my heart. Because of those evil people back their [sic], I was raised without a mother. But God will or has taken care of that."[5]

TRUTH ABOUT TRUNK MURDERS DIES WITH WINNIE RUTH JUDD[6]

In unfinished business, the Arizona Daily Star and other news sources reported the death of Winnie Ruth Judd. Used in this book as a comparison case to that of Arizona's Eva Dugan, Winnie Ruth Judd's death sentence was commuted on December 22, 1971. She had been convicted of killing her two roommates and dismembering their bodies. Some claim she took the blame to protect the man she loved. The truth will probably never be known. She died peacefully at the age of 93.

MURDEROUS DRIVER DIES ON NEVADA'S DEATH ROW[7]

Another death was that of Priscilla Ford who died while still on Nevada's death row. On Thanksgiving day 1982, claiming to be Christ and driving her Lincoln Continental, Priscilla Ford bore down on a crowded sidewalk in Reno, Nevada's casino district. After it was over, six people were dead and a couple dozen injured. She was convicted and sentenced to die. She "cheated the hangman" with her death on January 30, 2005 at the Southern Nevada Women's Correctional Center in Las Vegas. She still had appeals pending.

> "That was such a sad case. It was such a tragedy for so many people. The fact they had to relive that case appeal after appeal, her death will probably bring some peace to those people. She should have been executed a long time ago."[8]

I must also here add a caveat-others, following my research on executed women, have claimed to include names of other women executed but not included in my list. For each woman I have listed, I have obtained independent documentation rather than relying on lists or anecdotes without independent confirmation. Because of this, Dora Wright was not included in my original research. Since that time I have been able to document the execution of Dora Wright and she is included in this volume.

Others have listed Shellie McKeithen as a women executed by hanging in Pennsylvania on January 7, 1946. My research from original sources document that Shellie was a "He" and not a "She." Two other undocumented female executions not included here, but named by others are:

Ann Knight 10/13/22 Mississippi hanged
Pattie Perdue 1/13/22 Mississippi hanged

Neither of these has been included here since I have not, as yet, been able to confirm their actual execution.

Betty Lou Beets (Texas Black Widow)
"My Time Is Running Out and the State of
Texas Will Pick Up Where My Husbands Left Off. . . ."

Betty Lou Beets became the first woman executed in the 21st century, She was sentenced to die in Texas for killing Jimmy Don Beets, her fifth husband. She had previously been convicted of shooting her second husband. He was not killed. Additionally, she was charged but never tried in the shooting death of her fourth husband in 1981, who was found buried under the patio.

It was her contention that she was the object of "battered woman syndrome."

The body of Jimmy Don Beets was found wrapped in a sleeping bag and buried under a wishing well/decorative planter in the yard of their mobile home. While exhuming the body, law enforcement officials also discovered the body of Doyle Wayne Barber, her fourth husband.

At first she told police two of her children had committed this murder. As it turned out, her son Robbie helped bury Beets and her daughter Shirley helped bury Barber.

She spent her last hours writing letters and reading scriptures with the prison chaplain. She requested no last meal and had no last words. She did, however, send a final letter to her supporters written on the night of her execution [to be read the next day].

Dear Friends,

Today has started without me as a part of the human race. I now rest in the arms of my Heavenly Father inside his pearly gates.

Oh, how blessed I was to have you, how blessed I hope I've been to you, to try to show that his grace is all we really need. I never could have made it without our Father's love, without all your love and support. What our Father has brought together let no one tear apart.

My prayer is I've left this hard-learned lesson. Help the lost, impaired, disabled, battered, and for all who are in need, stick by the banner and carry it on. Help one another right where you are, near or far. Give your heart in all that is right and good. Bring knowledge to those who don't understand, that they can reach out and learn what they can do for themselves and others.

Always remember the battle is not over, but show up, put on the armor of God and let Him fight the battle through us. Then and only then will we win.

Trust that we all ran a good race and we won together. I'll leave this earth knowing I was loved by many. God is pleased and blessed that your faith was instilled in Him. His rewards are yours.

I love you all and will see you on the other side. God blesses you all. Keep faith and give all the glory to God.

Love,

Bettie[9]

[Her attorney had agreed to defend her in exchange for her signatures on a contract giving him all rights to her story and any books or movies made about her.]

Christina Riggs "Now I Can Be With My Babies as I Always Intended."

Christina Riggs, a licensed nurse, put her two children to bed. Justin, 5 years old and Shelby, age 2 were found lying next to each other in bed by their grandmother. Each had been poisoned and suffocated and, on the floor lay Christina Riggs who had passed out after leaving suicide notes to her mother and ex-husband:

> "I hope one day you will forgive me for taking my life and the life of my children. But I can't live like this any more, and I couldn't bear to leave my children behind to be a burden on you or to be separated and raised apart from their fathers and live knowing their mother killed herself."[10]

It was fully her intention to die but she was found, rushed to the hospital and her life was saved so she could stand trial for killing her children.

The defense argued she suffered from chronic depression and post-traumatic stress disorder, the latter brought on by her nursing work with victims of the Timothy McVeigh bombing of the Federal Building in Oklahoma City.

In spite of defense claims, the jury found her guilty. The prosecutor contended the children were an inconvenience to her and that she left them alone while she worked and attended Karaoke nights at the local bar.

Christina Riggs is one of the few women executed who really wanted to die. She wanted to be with her children as she had originally planned. On death row she corresponded with other death row inmates and did a lot of reading. On one occasion, using her nursing skills, she even saved the life of an inmate who suffered a seizure.

She filed no clemency appeal with Arkansas Governor, Mike Huckabee, although there were others who appealed on her behalf. One group sent a bouquet to a prayer service held for her. The bouquet consisted of white carnations–each representing a man executed in Arkansas, two pink carnations symbolizing Riggs two children and a red rose symbolizing Christina.

Christina Riggs was executed by lethal injection on May 3, 2002. Her last words were:

> No words can express just how sorry I am for taking the lives of my babies. No way I can make up for or take away the pain I have caused everyone who knew and loved them.[11]

After the lethal drugs were administered, her last words were, "I love you, my babies."

Her mother was not present at her execution. Due to a technicality in Arkansas law, she had to choose between visiting her daughter prior to her execution or

witnessing the execution. The law did not allow her to do both and she chose
to have the visit rather than attend the execution.

Wanda Jean Allen: "I Am the Type of Person I Will Hunt Someone Down I Love and Kill Them."

Wanda Jean Allen was one of the few women executed who had a previous
conviction for murder. In 1981, she had been convicted in the shooting death
of Detra Pettus. While serving 4 years for this manslaughter sentence she met
Gloria Leather. Leather was serving a sentence of 15 years for forgery and 10
years for larceny. The two made contact after their release and maintained a
stormy intimate relationship. The police had been called to their house on
several occasions for domestic disputes and in December, 1988, another argument broke out as Gloria was packing her car to move out. According to
prosecutors, Allen had sent a card to Leather in which she added a post script,
"I am the type of person I will hunt someone down I love and kill them." On
this day, that threat was apparently realized as Wanda Jean shot Gloria in the
stomach. Gloria was parked in the parking lot of the local police station and
seated in her car. Her mother was present at the time.

The defense argued Wanda Jean was "borderline mentally retarded" and
had "neuro-psychological problems." According to her family she had been
hit and ran over by a large truck as a child and suffered severe head injury.
Later, at her clemency hearing, expert witnesses would testify such injury
could affect her reasoning and impulse control.

This crime and the subsequent trial took place in the conservative Bible
belt and Allen's homosexuality, while not an explicit issue was, it was
claimed, an implicit thread running throughout.

In spite of Gloria Leather's mother's opposition to the death penalty,
Wanda Jean Allen was convicted and sentenced to die. She spent 12 years on
death row.

As her execution date approached, she made her final clemency appeal to
the Oklahoma Board of Pardons and Parole. While Gloria Leather's mother
had stated her forgiveness, the rest of the family was still bitter and argued for
the execution. Gloria's brother, Greg Wilson stated, "Let Wanda Jean Allen
go to sleep so we can go to sleep."[12]

And, another brother, after hearing Wanda Jean's appeal to the Pardon and
Parole Board state, "Please let me live. Please let me live," stated, "That's the
same thing my sister said."[13] By a three to one vote, the Board voted to deny
Allen's request for clemency.

Jesse Jackson came to Oklahoma in an attempt to influence Governor
Keating to issue a stay. He ended up being arrested for trespassing on prison

property. All his attempts were unsuccessful. Wanda Jean Allen died by lethal injection at 9:21p.m. Her last meal was a bag of chips and her last words were, "Lord forgive them for they know not what they do." Then she stuck her tongue out at the witnesses as she "went to sleep."

Marilyn Kay Plantz "She Told Us to Burn Him."

It was charged that Marilyn Kay Plantz manipulated two black teenage young men, Clifford Bryson (18) and William McKimble (18) to kill her husband, Jim. Plantz and Bryson were in love and planned to leave the state and start a new life together. When asked why she didn't just divorce her husband she told Bryson that Jim Plantz said he would either commit suicide or kill her if she left him.

Jim Plantz was attacked by the two boys with baseball bats as he returned from work on August 26, 1988. Entering his home whistling and carrying a grocery bag, he was beaten to death by both boys. His only sound was calling out the name of "Marilyn" for help. He collapsed on the floor and was still alive when Marilyn came out of her bedroom. Seeing the body, she stated it didn't look like an accident and told the boys to take him out and burn him. They drove out of town with the still breathing Jim Plantz in his pickup, poured gasoline on it and set it on fire. As they looked back, they saw him raise up and try to escape the blaze but it was too late.[14]

Eventually William McKimble plead guilty and received a life sentence for his testimony against Plantz and Bryson. Both were tried together and given the death penalty. Bryson was executed by lethal injection on June 15, 2000.

The Plantz' had two children at the time of the killing, Trina, age 9 and Christopher, age six. Marilyn had convinced her teenage lover that Jim Plantz was abusive and beat her regularly. When arrested he told police, "I didn't have no specific reason why I killed him. All I was thinking while I was beating him was all the times she came up to me with a black eye and crying. I didn't like that."[15]

Bryson and Plantz had made other plans to kill her husband but never carried them out.

This view of the Plantz' relationship was contradicted by a family member who expressed amazement:

"It's like when you hear people talk about the perfect marriage–they never argue, never fought, no cross words."[16]

Others attributed Marilyn Plantz' actions to boredom indicating she felt like she had missed out on the excitement of life because she got pregnant too early. It was claimed she would leave her children with a baby sitter then prostitute herself in order to get money for drugs. It was in this process that she met William Bryson.[17]

Her attorneys failed to present evidence she had been raped by Plantz prior to this marriage and that she came from a family in which she had been sexually, psychologically and physically abused.

Her attorneys appealed her conviction on the grounds that the work of Joyce Gilchrist, the Oklahoma City Crime Lab Director, was suspect and that she, in fact, was under investigation. It was charged that she had, ". . . misidentified evidence and given improper testimony."[18]

A spokesperson for the Oklahoma Criminal Defense Trial Lawyers Association (OCDTLA) stated:

> "If one juror was convinced to give the death penalty to Marilyn Plantz due to the testimony of Ms. Gilchrist, Marilyn should not be executed. . . ."[19]

This argument did not prevail as it was argued the testimony given by Gilchrist was not significant.

Marilyn Plantz' final statement, "What God has given me is love. I have overcome the world. Nothing, absolutely nothing, can separate us from the love of God." Her last meal was a request for ". . . a chicken taco salad, two cinnamon twists, a piece of pecan pie and two cans of Coca-cola."

Lois Nadean Smith "I Won't Have to Hear Her Name Anymore."

In high school, she was known as "Mean Nadean." In 1982 she and her 18 year old son, James Gregory Smith, tortured and killed his ex-girlfriend, Cynthia Lucille Baillee. She had been shot a total of 9 times, stabbed in the throat and stomped on. Some reports claim Cynthia was going to turn Greg in to local law enforcement for his involvement with drugs; other reports claim she was trying to arrange Greg's murder. Either way, Lois Nadean Smith took an active role in coming to her sons's aid. They picked Cynthia up at a motel and drove her to Smith's ex-husband's house. On the way, Lois Smith stabbed Cynthia in the throat and later, with her son reloading the pistol, "finished her off."

The trial was not of great interest. Son Greg, as an accomplice, was given a life sentence and Lois Nadean Smith sentenced to die.

The appeals process articulated some interesting arguments including:

- influence of drugs and alcohol
- below average intelligence

- first offender status
- past physical abuse
- brain damage from being hit by a truck while young
- inability to control violent impulses

None of these seemed to prevail and Lois Nadean Smith was executed by lethal injection. Her last words were asking for forgiveness, and her last meal was barbequed ribs, onion rings, strawberry banana cake and cherry lemonade.

Lynda Lyon-Sibley [Block] "Give Me Liberty or Give Me Death."

Lynda Lyon (the name she preferred) died in Alabama's "Big Yellow Mama" early in the morning of May 10, 2002. She had no last words and ate no last meal. True to her "anti-government activist" nature, she died glaring at prison officials as the switch was thrown.

Her odyssey to the chair included interludes as a cub scout mother, library patron, devoted wife and society climber. It ended when she and her common-law husband, George Sibley, killed Opelika police officer, Roger Motley.

While "on the lam" from an assault on her 71 year old husband, Lyon and George Sibley–along with Lyon's nine year old son, Gordon–were stopped in a shopping mall parking lot. Lyon was using a pay phone and George was in the car with Gordon. Officer Motley approached the car and asked Sibley for his driver's license. Sibley and Lyon had, because of their "constitutional" leanings, destroyed their driver's licenses, birth certificates and other official documents. Here the story takes two directions. The prosecution charged that Sibley drew his gun and began to fire at Officer Motley. Sibley claimed the officer reached for his gun and that he, Sibley, returned fire in self defense. Lyon heard the shots, drew her pistol from her purse and charged into the fight shooting at Officer Motley as well. Motley radioed for help and later died at the hospital. Lyon, Sibley and Gordon made their escape but were later surrounded and captured by the SWAT team as they sat in her red mustang with a bumper sticker that read, "A woman raped is a woman without a gun."[20] Gordon had been released to the officers prior to the stand off.

The trial was pretty much as expected. Lynda acted as her own attorney and challenged the authority of Alabama courts and its officers. In spite of her arguments, she was found guilty and sentenced to die. In a separate trial, George Sibley was also given the death penalty. They became the only husband and wife on Alabama's death row.

While awaiting death at Tutwiler Prison for Women, she carried on an active correspondence with supporters and others of the faithful. She spent her time reading and caring for her hair and nails. Her son, Gordon, went to live with his grandmother.

Juanita Motley had planned to witness the execution, She even showed up but asked to be escorted out after the curtain of the execution chamber was opened. "I went as far as I could with this . . . . I saw Lynda, but when they pulled back the blind to put the hood over her face, I asked the officer to take me out."[21]

The execution had been stayed from its original date of April 19. This was done since this date was the anniversary of the Branch Davidian fire in Waco, Texas. This was a significant date for those who shared Lyon's constitutional beliefs and officials wanted to avoid any implications of making her a martyr.

Lynda Lyon was another of the few women to be executed who did not fight her execution. She refused to appeal to the state of Alabama since she and George refused to acknowledge the state's authority. Lynda Lyon was probably the last woman to be executed in Alabama's electric chair. She died "stoically" on May 10, 2002 and was followed 3 years later by George Sibley on August 4, 2005, who died by lethal injection.

Aileen Carol Wuornos ("Damsel of Death")
"If I Am Damned, Who Is Forgiven?"

The story of Aileen Wuornos, "The Damsel of Death," is a long one–so long it has been the subject of three books, two movies, one opera and even a comic book. She has been called America's first female serial killer. Whether she was or wasn't can be a definitional issue. There have been other women who killed serially–several victims over a period of time. But, relying on F.B.I. definitions, Wuornos fit the profile of a serial killer because:

• She killed more than three people
• Targeted victims she didn't know
• Allowed time to elapse between each killing[22]

Wuornos killed seven men in Florida. She was charged with the deaths of six of them since the body of the seventh has never been found. She was found guilty and sentenced to die for all six deaths. As she left the courtroom, she screamed at the jury and called them "scum bags." At her sentencing she stated, "Thank you, I'll be up in heaven while you all rot in hell."

Her personal life ran the gamut from abuse as a child–physical, sexual and psychological–through promiscuity, prostitution, substance abuse and lesbianism. Her mother abandoned her and she was raised by her grandparents.

Her father, a convicted molester, committed suicide in prison. Her grandfather also killed himself. Her grandmother died of liver failure when Aileen was 15 and she lived on her own from then on.

Her longest relationship was with her lesbian lover, Tyria Moore. But, it was Moore who provided some of the evidence against Wuornos. The two of them drank often together at a biker bar called the Last Resort. Aileen was at this bar at the time of her arrest. The bar now touts the slogan, "Cold beer and killer women."[23]

Referring to herself as an "exit-to-exit" highway hooker, Wuornos confessed when she became concerned police were trying to gather evidence against Tyria. This concern was fostered by the police and Tyria who worked together through several jail phone conversations to get Aileen to confess.

At first she claimed self defense because the men were attempting to rape her. Later she changed her story and accepted responsibility for their deaths.

Her trial and the aftermath resembled a circus production. The investigators were negotiating movie deals, the media was dragging out horror stories, the myth makers were embellishing her life's experiences and Wuornos, herself, was telling morbid and conflicting versions of how she survived her past. A sideshow to the production was her adoption by an Evangelical Christian woman and her husband.

Wuornos eventually fired her attorneys and her appeals, stating, "I need to die for the killing of those people."

The night of her execution she could have ordered anything for her last meal that was under $20. She did not choose to eat but was given a cup of coffee. Her last words were:

> I'd just like to say I'm sailing with the rock, and I'll be back like Independence Day, with Jesus June 6. Like the movie, big mother ship and all, I'll be back.

Francis Elaine Newton "I know I Did Not Murder My Kids and My Family."

Francis Newton's story is a short one. She was arrested and charged with the shooting deaths of her husband, Adrian (23), son Alton, age 7, and baby daughter, Farrah, age 2 months. Police said her motive was the insurance policy she had just recently taken out on them (excluding her 7 year old son). Francis claimed the deaths were due to a debt Adrian owed to a drug dealer by the name of "Charlie;" that he had killed them as revenge.

Her story was that she and Adrian had been having marital problems. She had left the house to allow him to think about their decision to reconcile. She returned a few hours later with her cousin and found Adrian dead, shot in the head, and both of her children in bed shot in the chests. Her cousin would later tell police Francis had hidden a blue bag in her parent's abandoned house prior to returning home. Police later recovered the bag and found the murder weapon–a .35 cal. pistol–inside.

She was tried, found guilty and, because there were multiple deaths, sentenced to die.

Because of recurring questions about her trial, the evidence and her attorney, Texas Governor Rick Perry granted a stay just hours before her first scheduled execution. These included:

- Questions about the existence of other guns
- Evidence contamination including that of the hem of her dress where gunshot residue was claimed
- Incompetence of her attorney, Ron Mock, whose nickname was "Deathhouse Mock" because he had never won an acquittal for any of his 16 capital homicide trials.

Even her in-laws were uncertain of her guilt and were willing to testify on her behalf:

"We are the parents of Adrian Newton and the grandparents of Alton and Farrah Newton . . . We were willing to testify on Francis' behalf, but Francis' defense lawyer never approached us."[24]

On review, none of these were deemed sufficient to overturn her death sentence.

Francis Elaine Newton was executed by lethal injection in Huntsville Prison with her mother, father and sister watching. She had no last meal and declined to make any final statement before the lethal drugs were injected.

COMPARISON CASE: TIFFANY
HALL—"I WILL NEVER GET OUT."

While these eight women executed since the turn of the century were all "murderers," their crimes were significantly different. One crime was political in nature, one sexual, four dealt with the death of husbands and children.

All homicides are particularly horrendous–but the crime of one woman–who was not executed–was gruesome. To some extent it points out the capriciousness of our justice system and, on the other hand, the irony of making any claims about the purpose and role of the death penalty.

The two were as close as sisters. Both got pregnant as teenagers and Hall baby sat Jimella's children. Tiffany was the mother of two children–both girls. Her friend, Jimella Tunstall, had 3 children and she was pregnant again.

According to official reports, Tiffany killed Jimella in Tiffany's mother's bathtub and cut her abdomen open with a pair of scissors to get the fetus. She then wrapped Jimella's body in the shower curtain and tossed her body in a vacant lot. After the body was discovered and identified, the search began for her 3 children–DeMond (7), Ivan (2½), and Jinella (1½). Their bodies were found three days later. They had been drowned in the same bathtub in which their mother was killed and their nude bodies stuffed in the clothes dryer and washing machine in the basement of Jimella's apartment complex.

Earlier, on the same day as Jimella's death, police were called to the Frank Holten State Park where Tiffany claimed to have been raped and consequently delivered a stillborn child which she named Taylor Horne. She refused to go to the hospital for medical assistance and an autopsy on the baby turned up nothing unusual. While at the funeral for "her" stillborn baby, she whispered to her boyfriend, Keith Horne, that she had killed Jimella's baby, stolen the fetus and that the baby really wasn't his.

Horne was home on leave from the Navy to attend the funeral of what he thought was his child. He reported this confession to the police and Tiffany was questioned as to her involvement. It was determined the baby had been stillborn on September 15th at the time Jimella had been killed and three days before the bodies of the other children had been discovered.

It was Tiffany Hall's confession that finally led the police to the bodies of the three children. Hall confessed to killing Jimella by hitting her in the head with a table leg, cutting the fetus out with a pair of scissors and leaving Jimella in the bathtub to bleed to death.

Obviously, the prosecution was ready to seek the death penalty but in an unanticipated development, the prosecutor accepted a plea bargain in which Hall agreed to plead guilty to five charges against her, including four charges of murder and one of intentional homicide for the death of the fetus.

The key element of this unusual agreement was Tunstall's family who opposed the death penalty. Stating, "We are spiritual people," Sandra Myer, Tunstall's mother, said, "I'm going to have [to] deal with this the rest of my life. I'm going to put it in God's hands. I have to forgive her. We all make mistakes. We all will need forgiveness. Being a spiritual person, I have to find a way to forgive."[25]

Tiffany Hall was sentenced to life in prison without parole. When the judge asked her if she knew what that meant, she responded, "I will never get out."[26] Sentence was pronounced June 10, 2008.

I have not always been tempted to provide a comparison case to a comparison case, but in this case, I can't resist.

Lisa Montgomery, 16, was awaiting her execution for killing Bobbie Jo Stinette of Skidmore, Missouri. Bobbie Jo and Lisa both raised rat terriers and had met and communicated over the internet. On December 16, 2004, Montgomery left her Melvern, Kansas, home and drove to Stinette's home under the pretense of wanting to buy one of her dogs. Instead, she entered Stinette's home and killed the eight month pregnant woman and cut the baby from her womb with a pair of scissors. She then returned home and began showing the baby off as her own.

Upon being confronted by police, she later confessed and was charged with the federal offense of murder and kidnaping by taking the baby across a state boundary.

At trial, her defense claimed insanity. They conceded her guilt but in an attempt to save her life used what prosecuting attorney, Matt Whitworth, called the "abuse-excuse." Claiming she had been abused by her mother and sexually abused by her stepfather, the defense also argued she suffered a condition called "pseudocyesis" wherein a woman comes to believe she is actually pregnant. Lisa Montgomery, her attorneys argued, should not be executed because of her mental condition which influenced her actions.

After deliberating four hours, the jury failed to buy her defense, found her guilty, and in the penalty phase decided she should die. Today she awaits her execution on the federal death row.

Throughout my research and writing I have made a point of never taking a position for or against capital punishment. Stories such as those detailed here make it very difficult to decide who should live and who should die. While serving as a member of the Utah State Board of Pardons that possibility existed as part of my Board's responsibility. It is never as black-and-white as some would assume. Sentencing someone to die moves from the realm of knee-jerk reaction to intense emotional and ethical soul searching.

NOTES

1. *Security Management*, January 1, 2004.
2. *The Brother*, Sam Roberts, Random House, Inc., 2001, p. 484.
3. *The Augusta Chronicle*, August 31, 2005.
4. *The Orlando Sentinel*, March 12, 2003.
5. *The Atlanta Journal-Constitution*, March 12, 2003.
6. *The Arizona Daily Star*, October 25, 1998.
7. *Reno Gazette-Journal*, January 30, 2005.
8. Warlese County Assistant District Attorney, John Helzer.

9. http://www.wsws.org/articles/2000/exec_file.shtml.

10. http://www.clarkprosecutor.org/html/USriggs629.htm.

11. *New York Times*, May 3, 2002 p.A.22.

12. http://www.ccadp.org/wandajeanallen-news.tm, p.13.

13. Ibid.

14. http://www.clarkprosecutor.org/html/death/US/plantz711.htm.

15. Ibid., p. 5.

16. Ibid., p. 5.

17. Http://eotd.wordpress.com/2008/05/01/1-may-2001-%E2%80%998211-marilyn
-plantz/p1.612/2008

18. Ip eit.-www.clarkprosecutor p.4.

19. Ibid., p. 3.

20. http://www.clarkprosecutor.org/html/death/US/block775.htm,p.5. (6/16/2008)

21. *Montgomery Advertiser,* May 10, 2002.

22. *Orlando Sentinel*, October 7, 2002.

23. Ibid.

24. *Austin American-Statesman*, Editorial Board, September 12, 2005.

25. Http://www.bnd.com/news/crime/story/365299.html, p.3.

26. Http://www.bnd.com/news/crime/story/365299.html.

Part Seven

Clemencies and Commutations

> In some utopian age every punishment will fit every crime perfectly. Until then the power of clemency will be needed to set aside the extreme penalty where the law is inflexible and to weigh factors that judge and jury could not take into consideration.[1]

These words of New York's Governor Harriman reflect the responsibility felt by many governors who face the task of responding to appeals for clemency from those condemned to die. Some states administer clemency and commutation through Boards of Pardon and Parole, others do so through the office of the governor of the state.

Clemency, defined by one author as, ". . . essentially a matter of grace, a matter of mercy, not something anybody is legally entitled to,"[2] can take two forms. Pardons release the offender and, in essence, serve as an apology for whatever legal action has been taken. Commutations, on the other hand, serve to reduce the sentence. When those on death row appeal for clemency, they are usually asking for a commutation of their sentence from death to life in prison.

Historically, clemency has been capricious–by its very nature. Pilot commuted the sentence of Barabas to please the crowd crying for the crucifixion of Christ. Others have given in to other pressures–political and financial. In some governor's mansions it was customary to grant "Christmas pardons" to those inmates who had served well as household servants. In justifying this practice, wardens believed, ". . . even a few Christmas commutations serve to encourage good behavior and keep hopes alive for all long-term prisoners."[3] Some governors created scandals by selling pardons and commutations. Others, like New Mexico's Governor Toney Anaya, granted clemency on ideological grounds.

Prior to leaving office in 1986, he commuted the sentence of all those on death row to life:

> On this day before Thanksgiving, as we reflect on the gifts from God that we, as Americans, have been blessed with, as we prepare for the celebration of Christmas, the day when so many of us celebrate the birth of the one upon whose life many of our religious beliefs are based, I am dropping a pebble into a pond that will cause a ripple. A ripple which I pray will be joined by ripples in other ponds across this great country. Ripples that, coming together, will cause a rising tide.
>
> In an effort to focus attention on the need for effective and humane crime prevention efforts and effective and meaningful crime fighting measures, I have a few minutes ago signed five Executive Orders commuting the death sentences of the five men on New Mexico's death row to life sentences without the expectation of their ever setting foot on our streets again.[4]

In 1991, following the example of Governor Anaya, Ohio's Governor Richard Celeste, just 74 hours before leaving office, commuted the sentences of eight Ohio death row inmates, including four women–all African-American women. He commuted the sentences of Elizabeth Green (age 27), Beatrice Lampkin (age 49), Rosalie Grant (age 29) and Debra Brown (age 27)–who also was under a death sentence in Indiana. Each was commuted because, according to Governor Celeste, he found some mental disorders or mental retardation:

> None of the women on death row belonged under the shadow of the death penalty. We had a disproportionate number of women on death row in our state. All the women were black in a state where only 13% of the women are black. It suggests the fundamental injustice in the use of the death penalty.[5]

The governors who dealt with the women in this book were not so idealistic. Some had doubts about the effectiveness of capital punishment yet felt duty-bound by their oath of office to not interfere with the verdict of the courts. For many, it was obviously an easy way out–relying on legalistic and/or "respect for the system." Others struggled with their consciences yet chose not to alter the course of "justice." Obviously, none of the appeals for commutation by these women of the dancehall were granted. Yet, it is interesting to read the justifications and rationale used by those governors involved.

GOVERNOR MARTIN L. DAVEY (OHIO)– "WHAT WOULD I SAY TO THE MOTHERS WHOSE SONS HAVE DIED IN THE CHAIR?"

There are many who argue with some measure of logic in these days of equal rights, [1938] woman should be treated exactly as man.[6]

Thus wrote Ohio's Governor Martin L. Davey in his 1938 statement denying clemency to Marie Hahn, who was to become Ohio's first woman to die by electrocution. His statement continued, "I do not hold this view, because it seems to me that woman is cast in a finer mold than man."

Marie Hahn (the "Black Borgia"), who we have already met, was convicted by an 11 woman, one man jury of killing several older men. It was charged she would seduce them, get their money and send her young son to the drug store to buy the poison. When confronted with these charges, she explained, "I like to make men comfy."

There was great pressure on Governor Davey to grant clemency and commute her sentence to life in prison. Like other governors placed in this same position, he struggled with his conscience.

> Frankly, something inside of me has sort of rebelled against the idea of allowing a woman to go to the chair. I was brought up to respect womanhood and cannot escape the feeling that there is a little difference when a woman is involved in a tragedy of this kind.[7]

However, the governor felt he had to balance his personal feelings with the issue of duty and fairness, and decided to deny clemency stating, ". . . I can find no reason or excuse . . . that would make it fair to extend clemency in this case."

GOVERNOR CHARLES J. BELL (VERMONT)–"TURN MY BROTHER'S PICTURE TO THE WALL."

Vermont's 1905 execution of Mary Rogers, the first woman executed in this century, caused an early stir of conscience and put pressure on Governor Charles J. Bell. One of the state's heroes, Admiral Clark, was honored for his bravery during the Spanish American War, by having his life-sized portrait placed on the wall of the capitol building. As the execution of Mary Rogers approached, Clark's brother wrote the governor:

> Vermont is again threatened with the horrible disgrace of twenty-two years ago [the previous execution of a woman in Vermont]. The reputation and honor of the old Green Mountains is in your hands alone, and every true Vermonter believes in that highest justice that is the sister of mercy. Should this poor weak woman meet her doom Friday in a State where my brother has been so greatly honored, please face his portrait to the wall. Every real Vermonter would hang his head in shame before the world. Have the mercy of the Master, and may peace of the bravely merciful be always yours.[8]

Mary Rogers, who was sentenced to die for killing her husband, was hanged on December 8, 1905. The governor refused her request for clemency. When notified the execution had been completed, he said:

> I am much relieved to know that the execution of Mrs. Rogers was accomplished promptly, according to law, and without a hitch or unnecessary delay. It was a disagreeable duty I have been called upon to perform, but notwithstanding my private views in regard to the matter, I have acted in the interest of public good and according to the law-abiding sentiments of the people of Vermont.[9]

Over 30,000 women had presented Governor Bell with a petition requesting he intervene.

After receiving the petition and other appeals in his hotel room, he stated:

> I believe that I know the sentiments of the people of Vermont as well as does any person in this room. I see nothing to discuss and I know of no law that is not as much for a woman as for a man.[10]

The *New York Times* editorial on the date of the execution supported Governor Bell's decision, while acknowledging the pressures that had been brought to bear:

> "Justice," as the law of Vermont, . . . worked its horrid will yesterday on a woman who had committed murder. . . . Yet all intelligent people, we think, will unite in praising Governor Bell for the firmness he displayed month after month in refusing to interfere with the orderly process and execution of the law he swore to maintain when he took office. . . . Many men and women, including not a few of both who know that the governor's position and course were exactly right, have assailed him, now with hysterical supplication, now with frenzied abuse.[11]

GOVERNOR HUGHES (NORTH CAROLINA)–"IF HE DOUBTS, HE DOES SO IN HIS INDIVIDUAL CAPACITY, NOT HIS OFFICIAL CAPACITY."

Mary Farmer killed her neighbor with an axe and stuffed her body in a trunk. Sentenced to die in the state of New York, she appealed to Governor Hughes just prior to her execution, asking for clemency on the basis of insanity. His refusal was applauded in *New York Times* editorials before and after Mary Farmer's March 30, 1909 electric chair execution at Auburn State Prison:

> In explaining his refusal to pardon Mrs. Farmer or to commute her sentence to life imprisonment . . . Gov. Hughes assert[ed] that the pardoning power is not entrusted to the occupant of gubernatorial chairs to be used as a means of re-

pealing the law. . . .If Gov. Hughes has read the latest books on penology he probably has his doubts about the propriety of putting such offenders to death, but he doubts in his individual, not his official, capacity, and he knows that his opinions on the subject, if he has any, should be expressed in a message of advice to the Legislature, not in a pardon.[12]

Following the execution, the editorial, dated March 30, 1909, in referring to the execution, stated:

The horror of it bore most heavily, of course, upon Gov. Hughes, who could have prevented it by a few strokes of his pen–if he had allowed what were undoubtedly his personal feelings to outbalance his sense of official duty and his respect for the law.[13]

The editorial then went on to "editorialize" about crime and punishment:

That Mrs. Farmer was a product of heredity and environment, and from one point of view irresponsible for what she did, is doubtless true, but the same assertion can be made with equal force in behalf of every male murderer, so it amounts to nothing as long as capital punishment remains a part of our criminal code. . . . Meanwhile, as was long ago suggested to *messieurs les assasins*, an obvious first step toward the abolition of capital punishment is for *mesdames les assasins* to begin controlling their emotions.[14]

GOVERNOR WILLIAM HODGES MANN (VIRGINIA)–"I HAVE NOT CONSIDERED SEX OR COLOR."

On August 15, 1912, Governor William Hodges Mann refused to grant clemency to Virginia Christian, a black woman, who killed her older, white, female employer. In so doing, he stated:

I have not considered the sex or color of Virginia Christian because no distinctions are made by law. If a woman is not to be punished for crime just as a man is punished, the legislature of the State must so declare. It is not within the power of the governor to do so.[15]

GOVERNOR HERBERT H. LEHMAN (NEW YORK)–"THE LAW MAKES NO DISTINCTION OF SEX IN THE PUNISHMENT OF CRIME."

Governor Lehman is the governor with the distinction of dealing with the most female executions. During his tenure in office, three women appealed to him for clemency. After the 1934 execution of Anna Antonio, the governor, after "most painstaking consideration," stated:

> Appeals have been made to me to grant executive clemency to Anna Antonio on account of her sex but the law makes no distinction of sex in the punishment of crime; nor would my own conscience or the duty imposed upon me by my oath of office permit me to do so.[16]

Governor Lehman had two more opportunities to grant clemency on women awaiting execution and declined to do so in both instances.

Less than a year after Mrs. Antonio's execution, Eva Coo ("The Roadhouse Queen") appealed to the governor to commute her sentence. She had been sentenced to die for killing her hired man, "Gimpy," so she could claim his life insurance. Her clemency appeal fell on deaf ears and she died in Sing Sing's electric chair June 27, 1935.

The third woman to die during Governor Lehman's reign was Mary Francis Creighton, who was strapped in the chair and executed while totally unconscious. Mrs. Creighton and her co-defendant, Everett Applegate, were sentenced to die for poisoning Applegate's 300-pound wife, Ada. By putting poison in her eggnog, Applegate hoped to get rid of his wife and marry Creighton's 15-year-old daughter.

Because Mrs. Creighton had suffered various maladies while in her death row cell awaiting execution, Governor Lehman appointed a commission to examine her. The commission reported there was, ". . . no evidence of organic disease," and that, ". . . her condition is the reaction to the situation in which she finds herself."[17] Governor Lehman then made these findings public and declined clemency, making no further comment. Mary Francis Creighton was wheeled to the chair and strapped in–never having regained consciousness.

Governor Henry Horner (Illinois)–"In my desire to spare this woman the death penalty I have earnestly and minutely, but in vain, examined the record. . ."

Governor Horner, who had previously commuted sentences of three women about to be executed, denied clemency to Marie Porter. In his statement denying clemency, he stated:

> The law of this state provides capital punishment as the supreme penalty for murder. It does not provide one penalty for men and another for women. . . . In my desire to spare this woman the death penalty I have earnestly and minutely, but in vain, examined the record to find some mitigating circumstances in connection with the crime. . . . As Governor of the State of Illinois I have no right to amend the statutes of this state to read that the penalty for murder should not

apply to women. . . . Notwithstanding my views as to the death penalty as the punishment for murder, it is the law of this state and a law which we are bound to obey.[18]

GOVERNOR C.L. OLSON (CALIFORNIA)–"IF SHE WERE A MAN, MY DECISION NOT TO INTERVENE WOULD BE MUCH EASIER."

In 1941, Juanita Spinelli, who was awaiting execution as California's first woman to die in California's gas chamber, wrote the following letter to Governor Olson:

> . . . please forgive me and let me live. I know God will reward you because God has said take not the life of a sinner, but save and convert them . . . I trust you and the people of California can find in your heart Mercy and let me life (sic) and as I have said time will prove I did not do what I said I did. Please, Dear Governor, don't take my life. I want to prove to you that I am good at heart, but I have been beat and cowed all my life. I have had more kinder treatment here at the institution than all my life. I have mad[e] a God's confession to you. He knows I am not guilty of this crime, please believe me, I beg you.
> Yours Sincerely, Juanita S. 533[19]

Governor Olson had granted three previous reprieves but finally decided he could not commute Spinelli's sentence. In his statement, he said:

> I have given the case a great deal of study, in the hope that I would find circumstances justifying a commutation to life in prison. Perhaps that hope was extraordinary because of the fact that the condemned person was a woman.[20]

After indicating the interviews and observations he had made and conducted, he stated:

> She is a pathological liar; while she declares great love for her children yet she no doubt would sacrifice them if it would help to get her sentence commuted.[21]

Continuing, he said:

> If she were a man, my decision not to intervene would be much easier. But since the law does not provide for any preferred consideration to women, I do not feel that I have the right to discriminate in the exercise of the power of executive clemency.[22]

Governor Olson granted 126 pardons during his time in office–the third highest in California history, and at the time of the Spinelli execution, he had just been through a scandal dealing with his Board of Prisons.

GOVERNOR J. MILVILLE BROUGHTON (NORTH CAROLINA)–"THE ONLY PLEA ON HER BEHALF WAS THAT NO WOMAN SHOULD EVER BE EXECUTED IN NORTH CAROLINA."

Roseann Lightner Phillips and her boyfriend were sentenced to death for the axe slaying of their white employer. She appealed to Governor Broughton for clemency. His response was:

> The only plea for clemency on behalf of the woman defendant was based on the contention that no woman should be executed in North Carolina regardless of the crime. I cannot subscribe to this view. The law makes no such distinction.[23]

In addition to the execution of Mrs. Phillips, it was Governor Broughton who was faced with all those executions scheduled for the same day. He was forced to commute five of them. The other three executions, including Bessie Mae Williams, were allowed to take place.

GOVERNOR R.M. JEFFERIES (SOUTH CAROLINA)– "WITH WOMEN DEMANDING EQUAL RIGHTS WITH MEN, TRUE WOMANHOOD WILL NOT ASK FOR EXCEPTIONS FOR WOMEN."

In the case of Sue Logue, sentenced to die for killing a law enforcement officer, her neighbor, and a mule, Governor Jefferies made the following statement upon being asked to extend clemency:

> I think I have as high a regard for womanhood as the average citizen of the state may entertain. Such respect for womanhood directs me to review this case from the standpoint of justice and right without regard to the sex of the person involved. The administration of justice in South Carolina would become a mockery if one sex were exempted from the operation of criminal statutes.[24]

He continued:

> My high regard for pure, just, sincere and true womanhood makes me sure of my position when I say that a woman criminal is not entitled to any higher con-

sideration than would be accorded to a man. I believe this would have been true before the present generation which has seen the rights and privileges of womanhood greatly advanced. But now with women demanding equal rights with men, true womanhood will not ask for exceptions for women from operation of criminal statutes.[25]

Sue Logue had been sentenced to die for her involvement in a situation that began when her mule kicked to death a calf belonging to her neighbor and ended with eight people dying–including her husband and three others who would die in the electric chair.

GOVERNOR GORDON PERSONS (ALABAMA)–"I AM SORRY TO BE THE GOVERNOR TO MAKE THE DECISION."

Earle Dennison was executed for poisoning her 2-year-old niece while the child sat on her lap. Dennison then left the child dying in bed while she hurried off to make the last payment on the child's insurance policy. In refusing to grant clemency, Governor Persons stated:

> I will not interfere with the sentence. I am sorry, of course, to have to be the governor to make the decision for the first time that a white woman must die. But the child is just as dead as if the crime had been committed by a man. The law does not contemplate any difference between a man and a woman convicted of murder. God bless Mrs. Dennison's soul.[26]

GOVERNOR EDMUND "PAT" BROWN (CALIFORNIA)–"THE FACT THAT SHE WAS A WOMAN DID HAVE SOME EFFECT ON MY THOUGHTS AND FEELINGS."

Elizabeth "Ma" Duncan, who hired two hit-men to kill her pregnant daughter-in-law and was sentenced to death, made her final appeal to Governor Brown. He was in the midst of a bid for re-election, running against Richard Nixon. Governor Brown, interestingly enough, had a previous "peripheral" contact with Mrs. Duncan. While trying to sell some apartments he owned, she had agreed to buy them but was unable to come up with the money. In facing the issue of clemency for Mrs. Duncan, the governor wrote:

> The fact that she was a woman–the only woman sentenced to die during my terms as governor, and only the fifth woman ever sentenced to die in California history–did have some effect on my thoughts and feelings. I felt a great repugnance

about letting a woman die, as I suspect even the toughest death penalty advocate would.[27]

The governor came into office as an advocate of capital punishment, but, throughout his terms, he had become disenchanted with its effectiveness and was, at the time of Mrs. Duncan's appeal, considered an opponent. In ruling against her appeal for clemency, however, he stated:

> In spite of the fact that she was a woman, a person with whom I'd once had some peripheral contact, I knew that there was a time in all capital cases when I had to just let go, move on to other things. I was the head of a growing state, in need of new schools and public health programs, with an election coming up in a few months. I had to say to myself, "I've got lots of *good* people to take care of; I can't worry about this bad one anymore." And that's the hardest thing about running a state where the death penalty is part of the law—to be forced to think in those terms.[28]

Governor Brown's dilemma went deeper than merely the case of Mrs. Duncan. Throughout his term of office, up to this point, in 42 clemency hearings, all of which were men, he had allowed 29 to be executed and had commuted 13 from death to life sentences. One case that received the most attention was that of Caryl Chessman, who had been executed in 1960–two years earlier. Chessman, who did not commit murder, was convicted of "kidnapping during a robbery" and sentenced to die. He managed to stay alive for 12 years as he fought his death sentence, but on May 2, 1960, he died in San Quentin's gas chamber. Governor Brown, who failed to grant clemency, had been criticized because of his "callousness" and "vacillation" over the Chessman situation and Nixon was making it a campaign issue at the time of Mrs. Duncan's clemency appeal. Brown won re-election, but one wonders what role the political issues of clemency and the death penalty played in his decision not to commute the execution of Elizabeth Duncan.

GOVERNOR JAMES B. HUNT (NORTH CAROLINA)–"WE HAVE A STRONG SENSE THAT POLITICS AND DEATH HAVE BEEN MIXED UP IN THIS CASE."

The very next execution, after Elizabeth Duncan, was Margie Velma Barfield. She died by lethal injection in North Carolina's Central Prison, November 2, 1984. Her death sentence came as a result of a career of poisoning. She would eventually admit to killing her fiancé, her mother and two people she had tended while they were ill.

While on death row, she became known as "Mama Margie" for her ministrations to the other inmates. Her appeal for clemency to Governor Hunt was turned down. Some have argued that politics played an important role. The judge (a Republican) who set the date of execution, scheduled it for four days before the election in which Governor Hunt (a Democrat) was running for a seat in the Senate. The governor's aides were concerned that some of his more liberal supporters would be put off by the publicity surrounding an execution (especially that of a woman) that close to the election. Mrs. Barfield's friends and attorney voiced their concern saying, "We have a strong sense that politics and death have been mixed up in this case."

Governor Hunt lost his bid for the U.S. Senate and Velma Barfield lost her life. It would be difficult to tell the extent to which the two might have been related.

CONCLUSION

Since the time of President Harry Truman, every president has pardoned the Thanksgiving turkey. Yet, governors appear reluctant to grant clemency to the women whose stories appear on these pages. Each had his own motives, yet there were some basic themes:

- Political ambitions and situations
- Reluctance to interfere with established judicial decisions
- Inability to find mitigating factors
- Failure to justify gender distinctions

The concept of clemency has been a difficult one for many officials imbued with the power of granting such reprieves. However it is defined or packaged, there is a failure to understand that this power is one of mercy, not legal right or due process. Florida's Governor Bob Graham's perceptions of clemency as "ineffable grace," captures the true essence of this awesome power vested in state executives. His refusal to spell out and/or justify the clemencies he granted because, ". . . clemency would become just another quasi-judicial proceeding,"[29] protects the unchallengeable nature of this power.

Karla Faye Tucker's attorney was wrong when he challenged the Texas clemency system. Governor Bush was also wrong when he ducked his responsibility by falling back on legal/bureaucratic posturing. If he wanted to grant clemency–as a matter of mercy and grace–he could have. But, he didn't–nor did the others, under whose watch these women died. There is no second guessing, it was their right and responsibility to do as they did. It was exactly as Governor Harriman said:

> . . . I am convinced that mercy is no job for a committee. Sitting alone in his office with the ancient awesome power of clemency, the governor must take on the most difficult task of all: he must become the conscience of the people of his state.[30]

NOTES

1. Averell Harriman with Murray Teigh Bloom, "Mercy is a Lonely Business," *Saturday Evening Post*, March 22, 1958, p. 84.

2. David Von Drehle, *Among the Lowest of the Dead: The Culture of Death Row* (New York: Random House, 1995), p. 35.

3. Harriman, p. 84.

4. Governor Toney Anaya, *Crime and Capital Punishment* (Santa Fe, New Mexico, November 26, 1986). Copy in author's possession.

5. A&E, *Death Row Women*.

6. *Cincinnati Enquirer*, December 7, 1938.

7. Ibid.

8. *New York Times*, June 21, 1905, p. 2.

9. *New York Times*, December 9, 1905, p. 7.

10. Ibid.

11. *New York Times*, Editorial, December 9, 1905, p. F8.

12. *New York Times*, March 24, 1909, p. 8.

13. *New York Times*, March 30, 1909, p. 8.

14. Ibid.

15. *Newport New Times-Herald*, August 16, 1912.

16. *New York Times*, August 10, 1934, p. 1.

17. *Ogden Standard Examiner*, July 16, 1936, p. 1.

18. Copy in author's possession, January 19, 1938.

19. Copy in author's file.

20. *Sacramento Bee*, November 19, 1941, p. 1.

21. Ibid.

22. *Sacramento Bee*, November 19, 1941, p. 1.

23. *Daily Slatesville*, January 1, 1943.

24. *The State*, January 15, 1943.

25. *The State*, Columbia, South Carolina, January 15, 1943.

26. *The Montgomery Advertiser*, September 4, 1953.

27. Edmund (Pat) Brown, *Public Justice, Private Mercy: A Governor's Education On Death Row* (New York: Weidenfeld & Nicolson), p. 110.

28. Ibid.

29. Op.cit., Von Drehle, p. 190.

30. Op.cit., Harriman, p. 84.

Part Eight

What Must a Woman Do
to Be Executed?

As I write, this nation's death rows are receiving increasing numbers of women. Their crimes cover everything from the killing of their own children (one on his way to a visit with Santa Claus) to the killing, dismembering, and burial of transients. The motives fall primarily within the three Ps—passion, profit, and propinquity. How many of these women will actually be executed? It is impossible to say. Out of 64 women sentenced to die at the time I began this research, less than 50% still remain on death row. Actually some of them even died there.

There are very few patterns that explain what determines whether a woman will be executed or not. In attempting to answer this question, I used a list of comparison cases, developed to match executed women with women who were not executed—but whose crimes were almost identical. They were matched as closely as possible to the type of crime, victims, geography, and historical period. Some of these cases have been presented in the body of this book. Those factors that could not be documented as having a direct influence on whether a woman was executed include neither her race nor her victim's; her gender (how she was portrayed as a woman was more important than whether she was female); her crime (many crimes in the comparison group were far more heinous than those for which women were executed); nor the number or gender of her victims (women were not more likely to be executed if their victims were male). What did seem to make the difference were the following factors:

- *Nonexecuted women were more likely to admit their guilt and more likely to agree to concessions for their guilty pleas.* Righteously maintaining their innocence did not work to their best interest—regardless of guilt or innocence.

111

Martha Clift was offered total immunity for her testimony against Eva Coo, even though Martha was the one who did the actual killing. Madelina Ciccone of New Jersey, who killed her husband in 1913, was offered clemency for her testimony against her accomplice, Velma West (known in Ohio as "the Split-brain Flapper"), and was allowed to plead to second-degree murder in the 1927 killing of her husband. The same situation was true of Lorraine Clark and Effie Jowers, both husband killers. On the other hand, Eva Coo was executed in New York, having originally been offered the same deal as Martha Clift, but refusing to have any part of it. Martha Jule Beck turned down a last minute offer of commutation before her execution as did Ethel Rosenberg who was promised a deal if she would only tell the "truth."

- *There was little difference in the specific nature of the actual crimes, yet sentencing disparities ranged from execution to incarceration for periods ranging from 12 to 180 years.*

Sentencing disparities involved such factors as pressure from women's equality groups, the possible identity of powerful people involved or affected by the crimes, the status of the offender, and the politics of the commutation process itself. Women's rights groups were involved in appealing to the governor in both the Mary Rogers case (executed) and the Bessie Wakefield case (death sentence overturned). For Mary Rogers, 30,000 women in Vermont and Ohio signed petitions in vain. Using the rationale "If women had the right to vote there would be no capital punishment," the Women's Political Equality Club argued on Bessie Wakefield's behalf that women who don't vote should not be subject to men's laws. In 1913, Bessie, who killed her husband so she could be with her lover, received a stay of execution and her death sentence was rescinded in a second trial. In the case of Lorraine Clark (1954), she was allowed to plead guilty to the second-degree revenge murder of her husband because of the fear she would name important people in a wife-swapping ring should she go to trial. Velma West killed her husband in 1927 when he refused to let her go to a card party. When it was suggested she was having a lesbian affair, pressure from an "unrevealed source" resulted in a deal in which she was allowed to plead guilty to second-degree murder to avoid a trial of full disclosure. In 1940, Mae Walker Burleson got 12 years for the assassination killing of her ex-husband's new wife in South Carolina. Mae was the daughter of a former judge and received a recommendation for mercy from the jury that found her guilty of first-degree murder.

- *For nonexecuted women there was a longer period of time between their crimes and the carrying out of the sentences.*

Nonexecuted women apparently were able to use the appeal process to their advantage. In the instance of Bessie Wakefield, her death sentence was eventually commuted—five months after her accomplices had been executed. This idea is further emphasized by defense attorney Gerry Spence who said:

> [I] like to delay the process a little bit. Maybe people will soften up down the line. Maybe they'll feel better in a year or so, so that a little healing can take place and justice can do a better job. Let a little time pass so the initial anger can also pass.[1]

- *Personal characteristics were instrumental in either eliciting or revoking feelings of compassion and empathy for the offender.*
The Germans use a word "sympatisch" which connotes a certain empathy and liking for a person. Sympatisch is likely to be the difference between the execution of Rhonda Bell Martin (1957) and the life sentence of Nanny Hazel Doss (1955)—both poisoners of their mothers, husbands, and children. Execution probably hinged on the fact that Martin was cold, hard and unlikeable, whereas Doss was personable, full of homey quotes, and grandmotherly in appearance. Helen Fowler (1944), whose crime compared equally with that of Madeline Webb, was black, stocky, communicated poorly, and had little education. She was executed for killing a gas station attendant in New York. Madeline Webb (1942) was white, also from New York, a graduate with a bachelor's degree from Oklahoma A & M, and who also killed someone in a robbery attempt. She was given a life sentence.
Pregnancy probably saved Beatrice Snipes (1931) whose South Carolina death sentence was commuted by the governor 10 days before the birth of her daughter—even though her crime involved the killing of a policeman. Age saved Annie Mae Allison. Her accomplice, Bessie Mae Williams (executed 1944 in North Carolina), grabbed two 50 cent pieces off the seat of the cab while Annie Mae was beating the driver with a brick. Bessie Mae was executed because she was 18 and old enough to be an adult. Annie Mae was given a life sentence because she was 15 years old and still considered a juvenile.
- *Varying press coverage ensued with executed women receiving the greatest level of attention.*
It is interesting to compare the case of Martha Jule Beck (New York, 1951) with that of Inez Gertrude Brennan (Delaware, 1949). Both crimes involved luring lonely men, using them, robbing them, and killing them. Martha was extradited from Michigan (no death penalty statutes) to New York (with a death penalty statute) to be eligible for execution. Her trial was reported nationwide over a period of 3 years. Inez lured lonely men. In her home was found a bushel basket full of letters from men who corresponded with her.

She would offer marriage and when the men came to her farm, she would rob and kill them. She and her 15-year-old son were both found guilty of first-degree murder. The jury recommended mercy for the son but not for the mother. Both were sentenced to life in prison. While both trials were going on simultaneously, Martha's trial received front-page coverage and Inez's trial was written in only 11 paragraphs of the *New York Times*.

Similar trials are those of Ruth Snyder (1928), who received a great deal of publicity compared with that of Margaret Lemardi, whose scripted husband killing (1926) was virtually ignored. Elizabeth Duncan killed her pregnant daughter-in-law in California (1962) and was executed amid outcries and appeals all around the world. Alice Wynekoop (1934) and Clementina Corona (1962) killed their daughters-in-law and Blanche Dunkel (1935) killed her son-in-law, even sawing off his legs and dumping him in a swamp. None of these three women were executed nor did their crimes receive widespread publicity—such as no foreign appeal on their behalf and no movie stars at their trials.

It could be argued that a woman found guilty of criminal homicide and eligible for the death penalty has a greater likelihood of execution if she is perceived to have an extensive criminal history (although the actual criminal history of both compared groups was identical, with only one convicted recidivist in each group); if she fails to portray the expected societal gender role of a woman (crying, remorse, emotional outbursts, "natural" motherly affection, etc.); if she has an accomplice who is willing to testify against her; if her case has been widely publicized by the press and if the press has given her a derogatory nickname ("Tiger Woman," "Black-eyed Borgia," "Obese Ogress," "Murderess Without Tears," etc.). Because of the importance of pejorative nicknames given by the press, I have included them with each woman's story whenever they were available.

Critics of the death penalty point to the vagaries in selecting who is executed—for example variables such as income, sex, and race. All such variables play important parts with respect to executions in general. However, by focusing specifically on women, a clearer picture emerges. Before the full implications of the death penalty are known, more detailed study of executed women must be done. To fully understand *what* the death penalty punishes, we must more fully understand *whom* it punishes. Should we find that neither question can be answered with any consistency we may also find the death penalty to be a tool of exploitation—sexual, ideological, political, racial, and economic.

NOTE

1. Interview with Gerry Spence "Crime and Insanity." *The Constitution: That Delicate Balance*. Columbia School of Broadcasting, 1984.

.

Conclusion

Through my research I now better understand why these women were executed. However, I am really no closer to understanding why they killed. There is no pattern indicating their motivation. Greed, love, fear, retribution, dependence — all are partial explanations. I don't see them as beasts, animals or any of the other stereotypes that are implied by the nicknames given them by the press. For me, I like the explanation of the matron attending Anna Hahn before her 1938 execution in Ohio, "she was so human, so human."

It is that very humanity that intrigues me. Through their own stories and those in the press, as well as through their pictures, I have discovered and tried to share that humanity. For me this quality is best discovered through their relationships with their children. Although each of these women personally paid the price for her crime, I find it impossible to comprehend what price must have been extracted from the children. Most of these women were mothers — some of whom abandoned their children, some of whom used them, some of whom ignored them, but all of whom remained mothers to the end.

Historically, many executions of women were related to their motherhood and included many who were executed for infanticide — a serious violation of their role as mothers.

- In 1638, Dorothy Talbye was executed for killing her 3-year-old daughter whose name was Difficulty.
- Esther Rogers was hanged and gibbeted for killing her illegitimate infant in 1701.
- Sarah Simpson and Penelope Kennedy were hanged the same day, on December 23, 1739. Both offenses involved the killings of their illegitimate children.

These women and others were executed, it seems, because they were mothers and had failed to respect the lives of the children they bore (or, perhaps to reinforce the societal sacred value of motherhood). It is interesting to note the role of mother was considered so "sacred" that, should a woman facing execution be found to be pregnant, the execution would be postponed until the baby's birth and sometimes even commuted so the mother could care for the child.

- In 1735, Catherine Connor was sentenced to die for the crime of "carnal intercourse." When found to be pregnant, she was pardoned. A year later she was arrested on a charge of burglary and executed.
- Bathsheba Spooner, after being sentenced to die, protested she was expecting. Her pleas went unheard and she was executed July 2, 1778. The autopsy showed her to be 5 months pregnant.
- Anna Hoag was sentenced to hang in January 1852, for poisoning her husband with arsenic. When found to be pregnant, the governor delayed her execution until after the baby's birth. She was executed 6 months later on July 30, 1852.
- Beatrice Snipes killed a policeman and was sentenced to be electrocuted. Seven days before the birth of her baby daughter, the governor commuted her sentence to life in prison.

During most of the 1900's, death sentences for infanticide were virtually unknown. Rhonda Belle Martin killed her own children but she was never charged with their deaths. She was, however, sentenced to die and executed for killing her husband. It is interesting to track the executions of women through the historical shifts defining the roles of women and motherhood. Today, women again are being sentenced to die for killing their children.[1]

Motherhood could, of course, work for or against a woman.

- Prosecutors and reporters, in an effort to impeach character, made much of the fact that Anna Hahn (executed in Ohio, 1938) and Rosanna Phillips (executed in North Carolina, 1943) had illegitimate children.
- The prosecutors during the trial of Betty Butler (executed in Ohio, 1954) stressed that she had been pregnant at the time of her marriage, despite the fact her crime occurred 6 years later and had nothing to do with her marriage.

In addition to these considerations, there have been some interesting relationships between mothers and children involving the crimes for which the women were executed.

MOTHERS, THEIR CHILDREN, AND THEIR CRIMES

In most instances, the crimes of these executed mothers did not involve their children either as victims or accomplices. There are, however, some exceptions, as I have already noted.

- Irene Schroeder's 5-year-old son Donnie was in the getaway car after she and two accomplices held up the grocery store. Donnie's testimony was used to convict his mother at her trial. [Lynda Lyon's 9-year old son was also in the car as they were surrounded by police.]
- May Carey enlisted the help of her two older sons to kill her brother. She promised the oldest an automobile for his help. Seven years later it was the youngest son who implicated his mother and older brothers in his uncle's death. The oldest brother was executed right after his mother.
- Helen Fowler's daughter Genevieve was present when the "Sugar Woman" helped kill a man she had invited to her home. Genevieve attempted suicide by drinking Drano after being forced by the prosecution to testify against her mother.
- Dovie Dean killed her husband. Her son Carl was a suspect until his mother cleared him by confessing to the crime. She explained, "They told me it was either him or me."
- Betty Beets used her son to bury one husband she killed and her daughter to bury another husband she also killed.

Other mothers committed their crimes for their children:

- Mary Farmer killed her neighbor to obtain the deed to her property. This was done so Mary's 8-month-old son, Peter, would grow up owning property and not have to suffer the poverty she had been raised with.
- Anna Antonio admitted knowing two men were going to kill her abusive husband but did nothing to stop them, stating she cared only what happened to her children.
- Ruth Snyder and her lover, Judd Gray, killed her husband because she was concerned about what would happen to her young daughter, Lorraine, in the event of a divorce.
- Marie Porter killed her brother on his wedding day so as to still be the beneficiary of his insurance policy. The money was intended to help support her four children who still remained at home.
- Elizabeth Duncan hired two men to kill her pregnant daughter-in-law so her lawyer son Frank would return his loyalties to her.

- Juanita Spinelli went along with the murder of one of her gang members fearing, according to her account, her daughter "Gypsy" would be forced into prostitution. There was probably good reason for her to believe this, because another gang member had previously threatened to throw her 9-year-old son off the Ambassador Bridge in Detroit if she didn't cooperate in his scam.
- Mary Francis Creighton, along with her 15-year-old daughter, was involved sexually with Everrett Applegate who, along with his wife and own 15-year-old daughter, was living with the Creightons. Mrs. Applegate, because of her voiced suspicions of the illicit relationships, had to be eliminated before she reported what was going on. She was given poisoned eggnog concocted by Mrs. Creighton and administered by Mr. Applegate.

These examples of executed mothers show some of the various ways in which their crimes were related to their children.

MOTHERS WHILE ON DEATH ROW

Although these women have been portrayed as atypical females, lacking in "natural" maternal affection or any other of the redeeming qualities of their gender, with few exceptions they continued to function as mothers—even while on death row. The few exceptions include Martha Jule Beck, who gave her two children away and, when they were returned to her, threatened to kill them unless they were taken away again. Elizabeth Duncan, while clinging to her son Frank, had previously put three other children up for adoption. Barbara Graham, who loved little Tommy, had previously farmed out her first two sons.

Other death row mothers continued to nurture their children while awaiting death.

- Mary Farmer was allowed to keep her 8-month-old son in her cell throughout her trial and while awaiting death on death row. She and her husband were both convicted of murder but his sentence was later commuted. Arrangements were made later for the boy to live with his father's brother and Mary left a letter to be given to him by her attorney when the boy was old enough to understand.
- Anna Antonio spent her time on death row writing to her three children. She pled with her brother to take the children into his family. He did accept her 3-year-old son Frank, but the two girls were placed in an orphanage.
- Ethel Rosenberg carried on extensive correspondence with her two sons, Michael, age 10, and Robert, age 6, while she and her husband Julius were awaiting execution for espionage.

- Betty Butler painted and produced charcoal sketches, which she sent from death row, for her son, age 5, and her daughter, age 6.
- Rosanna Phillips, who had been raised by a grandmother and an aunt because her own mother was too unstable, arranged while on death row for her two children to be raised by her mother.
- Louise Peete, although a convicted recidivist, fought fiercely to shield and protect her only daughter from the publicity that surrounded her trial and ultimate execution.
- Barbara Graham swore on 2-year-old Tommy's head that she was innocent. She also did all she could to protect her 14-year-old son from any publicity because, "they are so sensitive at that age."

Some of these mothers were ignored by their children while awaiting death, whereas others received frequent visits and were given a great deal of support.

- Eva Dugan never divulged the whereabouts of her son. Her daughter wrote her only infrequently. Her main contact was with her aged father, who lived in California.
- Lena Baker's children suffered the stigma of their mother's crime and existence on death row. They distanced themselves from her and failed to communicate with her at all.
- Rose Marie Stinette was buried in Potter's Field because her daughter had no money with which to claim her body.
- Dovie Dean's relatives included her father, sisters and children. Despite family protestations of grief to reporters, none visited her in her last hours. A representative from the funeral home accompanied her body back to West Virginia for burial where, today, she still lies in an unmarked grave.
- Ma Duncan, after giving away three of her children, was supported by her son Frank throughout her trial and execution. He was pleading for her life with the governor of California at the moment the pellets were dropped in the gas chamber to begin the execution.
- Velma Barfield was supported by her children during her stay on death row. They helped with the appeals and tried to get her sentence commuted on the grounds the drugs she had used were at fault for her actions.

MOTHERS TO THE END

These executed women, considered the antithesis of motherhood, exhibited unusual courage and maternal protectiveness as they faced their pending executions. In many instances their children were still a part of their lives to the very end.

- Oscar, 12-year-old son of Anna Hahn, visited his mother just a few hours before her execution. On his way out of death row, he paused to answer some questions put to him by reporters. His parting comment was, "She is the best mother a person could ever have."
- Donni Schroeder, 6-year-old son of Irene Schroeder, the "Trigger Woman," visited his mother after seeing the governor of the State of Pennsylvania to plead for her life. Leaving her death row cell before her execution he told reporters, "I think Mom would make a nice angel."
- Lorraine Snyder, age 9, along with her grandmother, visited her mother Ruth Snyder just before her execution. Reporters had previously taken a picture of Lorraine kneeling in an attitude of prayer on behalf of her mother.
- Michael and Robert Rosenberg, although having visited their parents on death row, first heard of their execution while listening to a radio program at home. Michael had handwritten (actually copied) a letter to President Eisenhower appealing for the lives of his parents. "Please let my mommy and daddy go and not let anything happen to them. If they come home Robby and I will be very happy and will thank you very much."[2]

Among these women as they faced their last moments, were both the timid and the brave. Each woman faced death in her own particular way, yet those who were mothers most often thought of their children in their last moments.

- Irene Schroeder spent her last days writing her life history to be sold after her death to raise money for her son Donnie. She also left a letter to be given to him afterward. Ruth Snyder, Mary Farmer and many others of these mothers did the same.
- Ada LeBoeuf had been unable to have a last visit with her crippled mother. As she was led to the gallows, her final words were, "My mother! My mother! Oh, God, isn't this a terrible thing?" After her execution, her 9-year-old daughter, Liberty, stood weeping into the casket, having been denied a last visit with her mother.
- Anna Antonio spent her last days making a dress for her 7-year-old daughter's birthday. When the girl received the dress, she expressed hope that her mother's stay of execution would also be a present. Instead, Anna Antonio was executed on her daughter's birthday.
- May Carey was executed just before her oldest son. Both were hanged on the same gallows with the same rope. To the end, her son put total blame on his mother; yet the two of them ate ice cream and cake together for their

last meal and he comforted her during the lightning storm that preceded their executions.

• Juanita Spinelli was executed in California's gas chamber with pictures of her children and grandson taped to her breast underneath her dress. This was her last request.

It is the picture of Barbara Graham kissing Tommy good-bye that haunts me. I don't know what kind of love she possessed. I don't even know for sure of her guilt. I'm glad I no longer sit on my state's board of pardons where decisions of life and death are a part of the job description. This I do know, however: It is easy to judge in our minds, and from a distance. It is quite something else to know another individual's heart. I don't claim such knowledge. I only claim a deep tentativeness when it comes to condemning another person. Justice presumes everyone should get what he or she deserves but it doesn't provide a mechanism to ensure how that is to happen. An imperfect system can, at best, provide an imperfect justice. And what do we say when we are wrong? For me, Barbara Graham said it best: "Good people are so sure they are right!"

NOTES

1. Streib, op.cit.
2. Meeropol, op.cit., *We Are Your Sons*, p. 251.

Appendix

Chronological List of U.S. Women Executed in the 20th and 21st Centuries

Name	Age	State	Date/Exec	Method/Exec	Race	Method of Crime
Dora Wright	**38**	**Oklahoma**	**07/17/03**	**Hanged**	**Black**	**Whipping**
Mary Rogers	—	Vermont	12/08/05	Hanged	White	Chloroform/drowning
Mary Farmer	—	New York	03/29/09	Electric Chair	White	Axe
Virginia Christian	—	Virginia	08/16/12	Electric Chair	Black	Bludgeoning
Ruth Snyder	34	New York	01/12/29	Electric Chair	White	Beating/strangulation
Ada LeBoeuf	38	Louisiana	02/01/29	Hanged	White	Gun
Salina Gilmore	—	Alabama	01/24/30	Electric Chair	Black	Shotgun
Eva Dugan	52	Arizona	02/21/30	Hanged	White	Bludgeoning
Irene Schroeder	22	Pennsylvania	02/23/31	Electric Chair	White	Gun
Anna Antonio	28	New York	08/09/34	Electric Chair	White	Gun/knife
Julia Moore	—	Louisiana	02/08/35	Hanged	Black	Unknown
May Carey	55	Delaware	06/07/35	Hanged	White	Beating/shooting
Eva Coo	47	New York	06/27/35	Electric Chair	White	Mallet/automobile
Mary Francis Creighton	38	New York	07/16/35	Electric Chair	White	Poisoning
Mary Holmes	35	Mississippi	04/29/37	Hanged	Black	Knifing/burning
Marie Porter	37	Illinois	01/28/38	Electric Chair	White	Gun
Anna Marie Hahn	31	Ohio	12/07/38	Electric Chair	White	Poisoning
Juanita Spinelli	52	California	11/21/41	Gas Chamber	White	Knockout drops/drowning
Toni Jo Henry	26	Louisiana	11/28/42	Electric Chair	White	Gun
Rosanna Phillips	25	N. Carolina	01/01/43	Gas Chamber	Black	Axe
Sue Logue	43	S. Carolina	01/15/43	Electric Chair	White	Gun

Name	Age	State	Date	Execution	Race	Crime
Mildred Johnson	23	Mississippi	05/19/44	Electric Chair	Black	Bludgeoning
Helen Fowler	37	New York	11/16/44	Electric Chair	Black	Bludgeoning
Bessie Mae Williams	19	N. Carolina	12/29/44	Gas Chamber	Black	Stabbing
Lena Baker	44	Georgia	03/05/45	Electric Chair	Black	Shooting
Corinne Sykes	20	Pennsylvania	10/14/46	Electric Chair	Black	Stabbing
Rose Marie Stinette	49	S. Carolina	01/07/47	Electric Chair	Black	Hired killing
Louise Peete	62	California	04/11/47	Gas Chamber	White	Shooting
Martha Jule Beck	30	New York	03/08/51	Electric Chair	White	Shooting/drowning
Ethel Rosenberg	35	Federal	06/19/53	Electric Chair	White	Espionage
Earle Dennison	55	Alabama	09/04/53	Electric Chair	White	Poisoning
Bonnie Brown Heady	41	Federal	12/18/53	Gas Chamber	White	Kidnaping/shooting
Blanch "Dovie" Dean	55	Ohio	01/15/54	Electric Chair	White	Poisoning
Betty Butler	26	Ohio	06/12/54	Electric Chair	Black	Bludgeoning/drowning
Barbara Graham	32	California	06/03/55	Gas Chamber	White	Bludgeoning
Rhonda Belle Martin	50	Alabama	10/11/57	Electric Chair	White	Poisoning
Elizabeth Duncan	58	California	08/08/62	Gas Chamber	White	Hired killing
Velma Barfield	52	N. Carolina	11/02/84	Lethal Injection	White	Poisoning
Karla Faye Tucker	38	Texas	02/03/98	Lethal Injection	White	Pickax
Judi Buenoano	54	Florida	03/30/98	Electric Chair	White	Car bomb/drowning
Betty Lou Beets	62	Texas	02/24/00	Lethal Injection	White	Shooting
Christina Riggs	28	Arkansas	05/02/00	Lethal Injection	White	Smothered
Wanda Jean Allen	40	Oklahoma	01/11/01	Lethal Injection	Black	Shooting
Marilyn Kay Plantz	37	Oklahoma	05/01/01	Lethal Injection	White	Bludgeoned/burned
Lois Nadean Smith	61	Oklahoma	12/04/01	Lethal Injection	White	Shooting
Lynda Lyon	51	Alabama	05/10/02	Electric Chair	White	Shooting
Aileen Wuornos	46	Florida	10/09/02	Lethal Injection	White	Shooting
Francis Newton	40	Texas	09/15/05	Lethal Injection	Black	Shooting

www.ingramcontent.com/pod-product-compliance
Lightning Source LLC
Chambersburg PA
CBHW021829020426
42334CB00014B/553